To
Lauren,

As my editor, I try to use the best I can. As someone I consider, I will simply say that I'm glad you are.

It was nice finally meeting you and hope to see you again. Thank you for all your help with my book, including listening to me go on about it in the many phone calls. I felt a connection to you. I felt a connection with you and it was a good feeling. Meeting you confirmed that feeling.

Darryl

WHY I PRAY IN THE SHOWER

A JOURNEY FROM FEAR TO BELIEF IN MYSELF

Darryl Duke

Darryl Duke

INFINITY
PUBLISHING.COM

Copyright © 2009 by Darryl Duke

ISBN 0-7414-5310-X

Published by:

PUBLISHING.COM

1094 New DeHaven Street, Suite 100
West Conshohocken, PA 19428-2713
Info@buybooksontheweb.com
www.buybooksontheweb.com
Toll-free (877) BUY BOOK
Local Phone (610) 941-9999
Fax (610) 941-9959

Printed in the United States of America

Published June 2009

To my wife Sylvia

Thank you for staying with me as I slowly became who I am today. Although I never realized it in the past, I know now that this journey has been easier with you by my side.

IT HAS ALWAYS BEEN YOU

It has always been me
It has always been you
We decided before we were born
To be together as I believe souls do

And while we are here with each other
Living in this world we know
It is our decision to love
That will enable us to grow

Grow in our understanding of one another
And grow in our kindness and caring
So we can continue to be together
And enjoy the life we are sharing

But only when we finally move on
To the place we left to be here
Will we ever truly know why
Our lives we decided to share

I do have one answer though
That I would like to give
I believe my soul needed yours
In order for it to live

I Love You, Darryl

To my friends and relatives and every person I met who helped me to keep believing in myself while writing this book. I want say thank you.

INTRODUCTION

"Is there a God?" and "Why are we here?" are questions I've heard answers to many times throughout my life. Most of the time the answers came from people of faith who said there is a God and we're here to do His will. However, there were other times when the answers came from people without faith who said there isn't a God and life is what you make out of it.

Although I was never religious, I guess I always believed there was some kind of God who helps us in our lives and never worried about anyone's answers until I was forty-one years old. That's when, with everything going good in my life and with me being happier than at any other time I can remember, I started doubting this belief, and soon found myself full of fear and emptiness. With help, this soon seemed to pass, but as the next few years went by and doubts in my belief still sometimes surfaced and made me fearful, I sought out reassurance that there was a God who brought purpose to our lives. Now, at forty-four years old, although I'm still not entirely sure why we're here, I have reason to believe there is something, a creator perhaps, that will explain to me what life is about after I die, and I pray to it in the shower.

Through that time, I found that reading books on the subject of God would bring me some relief from the fear I felt and temporarily make me feel better. But because none of those books gave me the total reassurance I was looking for, I eventually turned to science for some kind of proof there was a God. Some of the things I read pointed towards there not being one and frightened me even more when they raised this question: "If there isn't a God, does life still have meaning?" However, as I continued my search for reassurance through science and acquired more knowledge about life and our universe, I finally became filled with hope in the possibility of a creator, and that question was replaced by these: "Does this creator I call God help us in our lives?" And if so, "Will it help me end the doubts I have and overcome my fears?" And right now with those questions slowly being answered, I not only have reason to believe in a creator, but I'm also beginning to believe in myself.

Sometimes, though, I wonder if the need for reassurance in a God really did start three years ago, or if it actually began the morning of April 27th, 1996. That's when, hung over and on the verge of losing my family, I decided to get sober and prayed to whatever God I thought there might be for help. When I drank, my life would slowly get out of control, and no matter how much heartache, sadness, or worry this would bring, I couldn't stay sober on my own. Once when I was 30, I even asked a former drinking buddy for help, because I knew he had been sober for a while. He told me the reason he no longer wanted to drink was because of the more spiritual lifestyle he now believed in. He also told me there was a possibility that I was an alcoholic, and that maybe spirituality was the answer for me too. I tried it, but after only eight months I decided to drink again—why? Did God let me down? Or did I let myself down? Maybe I just wasn't truly ready to surrender and believe like my friend did. Then, after six more years of drinking—and more heartache—came that frightening morning when I knew I would have to try again.

Today, I have a sense of serenity some days that makes me believe everything will be all right, even when it's not. I can also usually remain grateful for the good things in my life no matter how unfavorable my current circumstances may be. Also, I have a sense of confidence in myself now that I never had before. I do wonder though what has been different this time from when I tried to stay sober before. Has God finally decided to help me because I'm doing its will by sincerely trying to lead a more spiritual life? Or have those things come about because of my own will to create them? My hopes are that the answers to those two questions will unfold as I write this book and continue to achieve other things I want in life. For example, I want to try to love everyone even if I don't like them. I want to keep growing spiritually, and overcome my fears by believing in myself and God. I want to be ok with not having all the answers to why we're here, and enjoy the here even more. And finally, if my belief is true that there is a God to explain this life after we die, I want it to help me explain to you Why I Pray In The Shower. So if you're like me and never experienced a flashing light or sudden true conviction of the "Almighty," then read on. If you have also been searching for answers, then read on. If you are afraid and lonely, but don't know where to turn to, again read on. And, if you just want to be happy by having something to believe in, then please read on. This book isn't an autobiography, but it does contain the parts of my life that I feel helped shape who I am and filled me with the hopes and beliefs I have so far—ones that make me realize that although my journey from fear to belief in myself has been a long one, it's far from over as I now set out to find my own purpose in life. A purpose that I'm hoping will enable me to help other people come to believe in at least two things: That everything's going to be all right, even when it's not. And that there is indeed some kind of God, and it's ok to pray to it, even in the shower.

CONTENTS

1

Why I Pray in the Shower

Fear started in my childhood, grew in my teenage years, and stayed with me through my adult life. Although it has changed and mostly subsided, fear can still enter my life today and cause me unhappiness. The only thing that helps me with my fear is Faith. Faith there is something (rather than nothing) that created the universe and life for a reason. I call it God. And I pray to it in the shower. Several months have passed since I wrote the introduction to this book, and although I believe in myself even more now, I still turn to God whenever I need reassurance in my life that everything's going to be all right. I do this by simply asking God for the knowledge of its will and the power to carry it out, and for its wisdom and guidance. I then thank God for everything in my life, and actually tell God I'm going to enjoy my day, be happy, and not worry about anything. Finally, I finish by also telling God I love it, and that I know everything will be all right. This is how I pray whenever fear enters my life and makes me unhappy. Fear that I have because of doubt. Doubt that when things aren't going well in my life, they won't change for the better. And doubt that faith in God will help me get through it.

I should know better about having any doubts though, because the last nine years have shown me things will always get better and that faith in some sort of God has been helping me all along. The last nine years were spent using this faith in God to change doubt into hope, and hope into belief. Belief that everything will be all right even when it's not, because I know I will be all right even when I'm not. Today I know I can eventually stop feeling worried and afraid no matter what my circumstances are, not only by praying, but believing there's a reason for everything and that God gave me the ability to be happy—something I wasn't during most of my life because of all my fears and my drinking. Drinking that started in my teens, and didn't stop until I was thirty-six years old and had finally had enough.

It was on the morning of April 27, 1996 that I awoke from a dead sleep with my heart pounding, immediately feeling terrified and sick to my stomach. Terrified because I remembered the argument I'd started with my wife the night before, and sick to my stomach because once again, I had been drunk. Although there were many other times I had argued with my wife when I was drunk, and had woken up feeling worried and nauseated the next day, this time was different. This time I knew I had finally pushed her too far and that she was going to take our son and daughter and leave me. I also knew this time that, with or without my family, I would have to stop drinking all together if I ever wanted to live a better and happier life.

Before I talk more about that morning and what I said to my wife to make her stay, it's important for me to go back over the events of the day before to better explain why I knew it was time for me to stop drinking.

The day before was a Friday, and I remember the weather outside was warm and sunny. This type of weather always put me in a good mood, and that morning was no exception. As soon as I got to the electronics store where I worked as a salesman, I immediately began joking around with the other salesman and got the day off to a fun start. Not only was I in a good mood, I was also feeling good physically because I had quit drinking two weeks before and had started jogging. Now you would think that the last thing I would need to do is get drunk that night. But that's exactly what I ended up doing. I remember later that afternoon, I was putting together a TV stand, simply looking outside at the beautiful day, when out of nowhere the thought of getting drunk hit me. As always, this thought brought with it that familiar feeling of excitement that I loved, and quickly turned into an uncontrollable desire. What I didn't seem to notice at the time, however, was how the urge to drink had hit me so much sooner than it had all of the other times I had quit drinking. I quickly talked my coworkers into going out drinking with me that night, and then cunningly involved my wife so she wouldn't object to me going out. I called her and said all the guys were going out, and that they wanted us to go along. I knew if I presented it to her that way, she would say yes.

Everything went according to plan as my wife met us at the store right before we closed at 9:00 p.m., and in less than fifteen minutes, we were all heading to a nearby bar we liked. I couldn't wait to get inside and order that first beer. Just drinking the first one always gave me a feeling of anticipation and raised my spirits even more because I knew I was on my way to the buzz that I loved so much. The one that made me feel like I didn't have a care in the world and everything was going to be all right. The sad part was, though, that usually when I got to that point where most people might slow down or even stop drinking, I didn't. Instead I would get a "What the hell?" attitude that not only led to more drinking, but also allowed me to be the person I wanted everyone to think I was. Sometimes I was the "Tough Guy" who would tell embellished stories about fights I never really got into. Other times I was the "Funny Guy" everyone liked, joking around all night and acting crazy. Mostly though, it was a combination of the two, and I loved having a reputation for it because it made me feel important. I just had to be careful, because sometimes I could get a little too crazy and spoil the evening. To help prevent this, I would often try and keep track of how many bottles I drank, and then depending on the level of my buzz, I would try to slow down and pace myself.

That night, we all ordered something to eat and, of course, to drink, and began shooting pool. Later on that night, as we continued both of these activities, I was on my sixth or seventh bottle when one of the other drunken salesmen decided to start getting pitchers of beer for us to share. Naturally, I began drinking glass after glass from all the pitchers that kept coming, and soon stopped keeping track of how much I consumed. I didn't care anymore. My wife apparently did care, though, because she told me I was getting very drunk, and she wanted us to go home. Even though I knew I was definitely feeling the alcohol, I still didn't think I was that drunk, and I wasn't ready to leave.

My wife was never one to drink that much, and I could never understand how she could just have one or two drinks and that was it. I would often get mad at her for "not knowing how to have fun," and that was how the fight got started that night. I remember after she finally got me to leave the bar, I had no problem with her driving home, but I began yelling at her for embarrassing me about leaving the bar in front of my coworkers. I told her that I didn't like the way she always did this and the way she acted when I was drinking and trying to have fun.

I don't remember much else except what happened after we got home. I recall standing in the upstairs hallway of the house we rented and saying something to her about her not understanding me, and then, while in an apparent fit of rage, suddenly ripping my shirt off and the buttons flying everywhere. Of course I didn't care about this or the fact that my son was in his bedroom and that I might wake him up, and I continued to rant on about how awful my life was. After I realized my wife wasn't even around to hear all this and must have snuck up to our daughter's room on the third floor to get away from me, I got even angrier. I went up there and told her and my daughter that it was time for me to get out of their lives and live the way I wanted to.

I had, over the last year or so, tried to make myself believe that without the restrictions my wife always put on my drinking, I could be happier. Of course, I was obviously already drinking without any type of limits and didn't realize it as I went on to tell my daughter how her mother didn't understand me and never would. I then stood there, perhaps drunker than at any other time in my life and told my soon-to-be sixteen-year-old daughter that everyone would be better off without me. I don't remember anything else after this except going back downstairs, getting into bed, and passing out.

This was to be my last drunk, and another reason I pray today. I never want to lose contact with whatever God there is that I now believe helped me the next morning and saved me from the loneliness and misery that was my life back then—a life that, while not always lived in this loneliness and misery, still felt like it because of an obsession so great that I almost always chose drinking over being with my family and regretted it every time. So after waking up that morning with the impact of the night before fully sinking in, I laid there not only feeling sick and terrified, but knowing in my heart I was an alcoholic and that I couldn't go on living this way. I also knew that the only chance I had of remaining sober and hopefully not losing my family was to ask God for help and to go back to a place I had been to before: Alcoholics Anonymous. That's why, after praying, I got out of bed, walked outside the bedroom to where my wife was, and told her I was going back to AA. She didn't say a word as I simply turned around, went back to bed, and quickly fell asleep. Usually, whenever I'd have an argument with my wife because I was drinking the night before, I couldn't sleep at all, but this time was different. This time, because I had finally surrendered and no longer wanted the life I had created using alcohol, I felt relief.

That morning was the beginning of the sobriety I still enjoy today, and the beginning of turning doubt into hope. At the time, my hope was that I could stop drinking for good and that I wouldn't lose my family, but now my hope is that I can help other alcoholics and anyone else who has doubts and fears in their lives that make them unhappy. People do whatever they can to try to be happy, but they really just need to learn how to love themselves enough to be happy with who they are. Alcoholics Anonymous and The Twelve Steps helped me to change as a person and become happy in my life. But more importantly, this is about how my journey from fear to a belief in a creator, and then myself, has helped me to become happy with who I am.

Almost all my life, I tried to be someone I wasn't because I wasn't happy with who I was. As a child, I was a frightened little boy watching my parents fight. Later on in life, I was a skinny teenager full of fears and insecurities. After my teens, I was an immature twenty-year-old man with a wife and baby who ran away from his fears and became a drunk. And only a few years later, I was an alcoholic with even more fears and insecurities who didn't like or love myself and would remain miserable for years to come. Thankfully, I stopped drinking and eventually started to love myself, but if it weren't for my search for reassurance in some kind of God, I may never have become who I am today—someone who feels love for others and tries hard to be a good person. Someone who is honest about his emotions and is not afraid to talk about them or ashamed to cry because of them. And someone who now simply wants to tell people how his search also changed his beliefs about life and inspired him to share them with others. I'm not asking you to believe what I do, but just know that my beliefs have made a difference in my life. I'm not trying to be perfect, whatever that is, but I do believe I'm growing spiritually as I try to be a better person than I was before. I still do things that I don't like myself for, but I believe that a part of spiritual growth is knowing you will always need to grow. I'm not trying to be like some of the people you see who claim to have all the answers to people's troubles. I'm just simply someone who has learned that by having faith, and using the tools of prayer, people, and hope to help us, we can find our own answers in life, and truly can create our own happiness.

The type of faith I talked about in the beginning of this chapter is in something I call God, something that will always be there to guide us and help us to believe in ourselves as long as we don't let doubt and fear stand in our way. I once read that all of our fears are learned except for two that we're born with—the fear of falling and the fear of loud noises. Maybe the one of falling comes from not feeling secure, and the one of loud noises is just a fear of the unknown, I don't know. What I do know is that as I go through life today, although I may not always feel secure, I can feel less afraid by remembering it's actually those times that make me grow stronger. And even though loud noises can still scare me, fear of the unknown is starting to scare me less. As far as any learned fears? They started in my childhood, grew into my teenage years, and stayed with me through my adult life. The only thing that I have found that helps me with my fear is faith. Faith in a creator I didn't have most of my adult life. Faith in myself I never had in my teenage years. And faith that everything was going to be all right even when it wasn't, which I so desperately needed in my childhood.

2

Why I Became an Emotionally Troubled Teen

When I tell you about some of the memories of my childhood, you may not think it would have caused me many emotional problems. I was never sexually or physically abused by anyone in my family, and actually had two parents that loved me. As a matter of fact, I can even remember back when I was four years old, my mom would tell me she loved me all the time. I also remember going places with my dad at that age. He loved taking me with him wherever he went, and although he didn't say he loved me as often as my mom, he did show it. I was an only child, and he spoiled me rotten by buying me toys all the time. So how did I become an emotionally troubled teenager if my childhood seemed so good?

Well, let me tell you about some other memories I have. The fights would start between my parents and my dad would yell, "You whore! Why don't you go back to Butchy Boy if you're not happy?" I guess this was a nickname for an old boyfriend of hers, and according to my dad, she had many. I don't recall my mom's answer, but I do remember her cursing and always yelling back. I also remember the range of emotions I went through when the fights first started. One minute I was upstairs in my playroom, contentedly playing with my toys, and the next one I was feeling anxious and afraid. Every scream I heard made me wonder how far it would go this time and if it would escalate to the point of my dad threatening to hit my mom, which it usually did. I would dread what might come next—both of them getting physically violent. Most often it was just them pushing and slapping each other, but it always led to the same conclusion. Me, a four-year-old little boy, running to the rescue, crying and yelling for them to please stop. I was so full of terror; I would often even get in between them in hopes of making them stop. To see and hear such horrible fights left an impression.

These fights continued for many more years to come, much in the same pattern. Their voices slowing getting louder, yelling and name calling, and at the very least, a threat of physical violence from my dad. Like the time we were driving home from my grandmother's house. I was around seven at the time, and once again my parents started arguing about something. Within minutes it got worse as my mom called my dad a name, ("Bastard" was the one I remember her using often) and then slapped him. My dad immediately pulled the car over, grabbed her arm, and told her if she tried it again, he would "beat the living hell out of her." She asked him if that would make him feel like a big man doing that in front of his son. I remember him answering her back and saying he would wait until another time to beat the shit out of her. She then threatened to leave him if he ever tried that (I guess getting hit or slapped wasn't enough reason to leave, but getting beat up was).

This gave me two things to worry about: the threat my dad made about beating her up, and the one my mom made about leaving. Both those fears would increase a few years later when my mom actually did go to a lawyer to see about a divorce and my dad found out. I remember that evening vividly. It started with my dad answering the phone, and my mom standing there listening to the conversation. I was sitting in front of the TV, not really paying attention until he hung up and asked her where she was today. No sooner did she get out the word "nowhere," before she was on the floor after being called a liar and him saying he knew where she really was. That's when two things became clear to me. One, my dad had just hit my mom so hard that she fell to the floor. And two, she did indeed go somewhere that day; an attorney's office.

I began crying immediately after all this happened, and then got hysterical as my mom got up off the floor and started fighting back. It didn't escalate though; I believe my hysteria caused my dad some pause about hitting her again and he just fended her off instead. After that, it simmered down to them just arguing about the whole thing, and then finally only silence. This was just the calm before the storm, however. I finally calmed down, and my mom was sitting in the kitchen smoking. My dad was getting ready to take a shower, and right before he went into the bathroom, he took my mom's car keys and told me if she tried to leave to yell for him. (Can you imagine telling your son to watch his mother so she doesn't leave?) Although my mom made some remark about this, the drama didn't start again until later, after he got in the shower. I was once again watching TV, only this time from our couch, when my mom walked up behind me and whispered in my ear she was going to leave. I looked up at her and saw what was obviously a spare car key in her hand, and my heart started racing as it sank in that she really was leaving. I then jumped off the couch, yelled to my dad (as instructed) that she was going, and followed her out the door, crying and pleading for her to stay. She, of course, didn't listen, and hurriedly went towards her car with me following right beside her. Within seconds she was there and opened the car door and got in, but when she went to pull the car door shut, I stopped her by pushing against it every time she tried. After two or three quick attempts at it, she yelled at me to stop, then momentarily gave up herself and started the car instead.

This was only a short break in the action though, because soon, she started the car. She yelled at me to get back, and when I did, she once again reached for the car door, this time slamming it shut. By then my dad had already come running out of the house with just his pants on, and when my mom started to drive away, he quickly jumped in his own car and followed in hot pursuit right behind her. (Yes, this story even has a car chase.) I just stood there crying and feeling very afraid as I watched them race up the street, wondering what might happen next. Would he catch her? And if he did, maybe even kill her? (This only came to mind because I remembered my dad threatening it once when they argued before.) Or would she get away and never come back? Finally, after standing there crying and thinking those frightening thoughts, I decided to go to a neighbor lady's down the street for help. I knew she and her husband argued a lot and I thought she might know what I should do. (He was an alcoholic that later quit drinking and someone who I eventually formed a friendship with.) I remember standing on the front porch of their house pounding on the door, hoping she would answer. When she eventually did, I began crying even harder, and slowly sobbed out what had just happened. I'll never forget what this woman did for me: she took me inside and hugged me to calm me down, and then did her best to reassure me that everything would be all right.

Later that evening, both of my parents did return home, but it would be a very long time before anything was all right. Despite this incident, there are a few more good memories of my childhood I still hold onto. Like the Christmas Eves when I would go with my parents to some of our relatives' homes and play all night with my cousins. And of course the Christmas mornings when I would wake up extra early, and my mom and dad would watch me excitedly open up all my gifts. Then there were the Easter Sundays filled with candy and a trip to Grandpa's house for dinner that I always looked forward to.

The best memory I have of my childhood, though, is going to Atlantic City for vacation; it was quite a different place in the sixties without the casinos. I remember as soon as my parents got finished checking into the hotel, they would take me straight to the boardwalk to satisfy my eagerness. It had many of the things that most boardwalks do today, like games, food, and all kinds of stores, but it also had a peanut shop that I remember for two reasons. You could always smell the scent of fresh roasted peanuts from yards away, and if you liked, you could meet the famous Mr. Peanut—a guy dressed up in a peanut suit. He would stand outside the shop with his cane, and I never failed to run up and say hello to him. There were also a few piers that ran off the boardwalk out into the ocean. Some of the piers had rides on them, like The Wild Mouse, which was basically a one-car roller coaster, and my dad's and my favorite ride.

One pier in particular, though, was different, and I enjoyed going on it more than anything else we did while in Atlantic City. It was called The Steel Pier, and I just loved it. So did a lot of people I suppose, because it had a song written about it that at one point in time played a lot on the radio. It also had a chicken that would dance to music for food, movies you could go see, and an outdoor ocean show at the end of the pier. This show included a seal act, diving clowns that were funny to watch, and even a diving horse. There was so much to see and do for families there, and one of my favorite things to do was to get on something called The Diving Bell. It was named that because it went to the bottom of the ocean and resembled a bell. I remember it only held a few people and had rounded windows you could look through. I also remember after it was finished descending to the bottom of the ocean, maybe 20 feet or so, I would get on my tiptoes and look outside one of the windows in hopes of seeing a shark. The best part of this adventure, though, came at the end when the operator of The Diving Bell finished telling everyone facts about the ocean. That's when he would say it was time to return to the surface and to please hold on tight to the rails in front of you. Then, when everyone was ready, he pushed a button and The Diving Bell would quickly spring back up to the top of the water, and almost all the way out, before falling back down a few feet under again. This made your stomach feel like it had butterflies in it, which I loved, and it then repeated this a few more times, but with less motion and less butterflies, until it finally settled at its original starting place.

As much as I enjoyed those times on The Steel Pier with my mom and dad, it wasn't enough to make up for all the other times that filled me with fear and sadness. Today, I still love my parents and have truly forgiven them. They have changed a lot over the years and feel bad about the fighting they did back then. However, they will never understand how it affected me. When I was in grade school and beyond, the fears that I experienced in my childhood would become more extreme and begin to affect me in other ways. As a result of my parents fighting, an uncertainty began to develop in my life. I never knew when an argument would start, how bad it would get, or even when it would end. I would worry about the outcome, feel angry at my parents for fighting, and eventually just feel very sad.

Even with all the fighting going on at home between my parents, I don't seem to recall having any specific emotional troubles through elementary school, but I did get into trouble more than most of the other kids. I also remember feeling that none of my teachers liked me, except maybe my fourth grade teacher. I think he knew I had problems at home and was very kind to me. If there was one indication, though, that something was wrong, it would have to be the fistfights I had all through elementary school. Actually, I can even remember having a fight as early as kindergarten and being encouraged by the person that walked me there in the mornings. This was someone who was like a brother to me and would have an even bigger influence on me when I was a teenager. It was my dad's younger brother, and he believed like my dad that even if you're scared, you don't run away from a fight. I guess I too inherited that way of thinking, but obviously took it to a whole other level in grade school.

Besides the childhood brawls, there were phone calls from school to my parents when I misbehaved, and a few parent-teacher meetings when the teachers reported I wasn't doing as well as I could in some of my subjects. Any fears or negative emotions I had were not overwhelming, but I do remember having them. Like the time when my fifth grade teacher called our house one Friday evening just after my parents and I had returned home from shopping. My dad bought me a Fort Apache play set that night, which included Calvary Men and Indians, and I couldn't wait to get home and play with it. Finally, there I was in my bedroom, getting everything out of the box, excited and happy, when the phone rang. I could tell by the conversation it was my teacher, and I knew she was telling my dad how I had been misbehaving in her class, and about a fight I got into with another kid. I had actually forgotten about her threat of calling my parents, but now here it was. At first, I remember being scared, because I knew I would be in trouble, but then this terrible feeling of sadness came over me, and I began crying. I felt that my night had been ruined and as the sadness stayed with me, I also got angry and began to put everything away before my dad even got off the phone. It turned out he wasn't too mad, but I did have to go to bed early that night.

So while I'm sure these emotions played a part in my behaviors those first six years of school, nothing seemed too much out of the ordinary. As a matter of fact, between the time I started sixth grade in the fall of 1971 and finished the school year, the fistfights had subsided. Unfortunately, however, this wouldn't last, and over the next three years, while attending middle school, I would do a lot more than just get into fights. I began my first year of middle school as a seventh grader in September of 1972. For the first three months of that year, I basically just joked around in class to get attention, and would sometimes receive paddlings for it by the principal. I hated getting my butt smacked, but I loved showing off and making the other kids laugh so much that it didn't slow down my classroom antics.

Then in December I turned 13 and started getting into fights again. This not only gave me the attention I craved, but also the beginning of a reputation. I was known as a tough guy who could fight, and it made me feel good about myself. Some of the fights were after school, but a few were in school as well, and one got me in more trouble than I bargained for. It began during lunchtime in the school lobby when for no particular reason, I decided to start a fight with this one kid. At first he didn't want to fight me, but when I kept on picking on him, he finally got mad and threw a punch. Since I knew how to fight, I easily ducked it and then threw my own punch, which struck my target. By this time, the small crowd that had gathered when I first started the fight had quickly grown, and before another punch was thrown, a teacher intervened and broke it up. He then took us both down to the office, where upon hearing from the other kid that I had started the fight, the principal gave me a three-day out-of-school suspension and called my dad to come and get me.

This was only the beginning of future troubles, however, because soon I would learn how to smoke and then, of course, smoke in school, and eventually get caught. One day I was in the school lavatory between classes and just after everyone else finished their cigarettes and left to go to their next class, I decided to stay behind and finish up my cigarette in one of the door-less toilet stalls. I heard the bathroom door open, and immediately thought it could be a teacher. For some reason though, instead of just throwing the cigarette in the toilet and flushing it down, I decided to cup it in my right hand and then put my hand inside the jacket pocket of my blue parka and take my chances. I quickly peeked out of the toilet stall to see who it was, and sure enough, it was a teacher. By this time, all I could manage was a nod, a faint hello and smile. In an instant, he was right there at the stall, checking behind me to see if I did throw a cigarette in the toilet. I tried to go around him and make my escape, but when I did, he grabbed my right bicep and held me there. I knew this teacher didn't like me, and my heart was racing as I stood there frozen, hoping he didn't realize I was hiding a lit cigarette in my pocket.

"What are you doing in here?" he asked. "Nothing," I replied. He waited awhile before saying anything else and just stood there holding my arm and smiling. "What's in your pocket?" he wanted to know. "Nothing," I replied again. "Get of out here," he said, still grinning. I started to pull away from his hold on my arm, thinking he really meant get out of there, but instead he grabbed me tighter, and said, "I didn't mean leave." In a matter of seconds, I went from feeling relieved, thinking I had fooled him and was free to go, to feeling uncertain, and then just plain fear, as he asked sarcastically, "Do you think I don't know you have a cigarette in your pocket, Duke?" I stood there, frozen by his question; something told me he really didn't want an answer, so I didn't say a word. He said he knew I had a cigarette in my pocket, because after he grabbed me by the arm, he could smell the smoke coming out of my jacket. Finally, he released my arm, commanded me to "throw it in the toilet," and stood there in silence with me. For some reason, this gave me a small feeling of hope that he might actually give me a break and let me go—until he said. "Let's go down to the office."

Although I had heard these words before, this time they really frightened me. I knew I would get suspended again and that my mom and dad would now know that I smoked. Even with those thoughts running through my mind, I still couldn't stop thinking how this would add to my reputation and help me be the cool person I wanted everybody to think I was, despite my insecurities. My latest worry was about my weight—I was so much thinner than all the other kids my age. Although I was considered good-looking and knew it, being so skinny made me feel self-conscious. I was also emotionally immature. I would always worry about what the other kids thought of me, and really wanted them to like me. I got very angry and defensive at the slightest critical remarks. And finally, the sadness that I experienced at this time would often deepen into self-pity. I never truly felt like I fit in with any of the other kids, which made me feel lonely. Coincidentally, most alcoholics will also tell you about the pure loneliness they felt from feeling like they never fit in with anyone either. I was already feeling this way back then, and the reputation I was trying so hard to have certainly didn't help, because it kept the so-called "good kids" from wanting to be around me, and the only kids that didn't seem to mind my reputation were the ones that also got into trouble or did drugs. Of course, I didn't feel like I fit in with them either, but at least I could call them friends.

Unfortunately, because of these friendships, it wouldn't be long before I found out something that would temporarily help me feel like I fit in. Drugs. They also made me feel good when doing them and I don't remember ever passing up a chance to get high. When I began seventh grade, the only guys I knew were the ones who lived in my neighborhood. Although I did hang around with some of them through grade school, only one or two of them were still my friends by this time, but I felt even they didn't like me. I also knew some girls from the neighborhood who I had become friends with. I first met them at the school bus stop, and after some initial shyness, began talking with them. I knew these girls weren't interested in me as a boyfriend, but they would tell me I was cute, and I could tell they liked me. This naturally made me feel good about myself, and I really liked being around them. Sadly, some of them would begin to feel differently about me when, later that year, I began acting like a tough guy. Although this really hurt my feelings, it wouldn't stop me from continuing to act like this.

The smoking and the fighting would be the beginnings of how I would try to be something I wasn't. I started going to the mall with a few of the girls from the bus stop and hanging around with these two older guys they knew from our neighborhood. These guys knew each other and went to the same school I did. One was a tough guy that smoked marijuana and never missed a chance to start a fight, while the other one was more reserved and not only smoked pot, but sold it too. It didn't take long before I was smoking cigarettes in school with them—and eventually also getting high with them by smoking marijuana. Thankfully, although I had some close calls, I never got arrested for it, or for that matter, anything else we did together that was illegal; let's just say there were a few times when I was in places I shouldn't have been in. There were many other times, though, when my older friends were off doing things I wasn't allowed to do, like going to concerts or late night parties, and I was left all alone.

The reputation that meant so much to me in school made the kids in my neighborhood want to stay away from me, and all the girls I knew had boyfriends. Not having any friends only fueled the insecurities and feelings of sadness I had, but my parents just didn't pick up on them. Here I was, a thirteen-year-old getting into trouble at school by fighting and smoking, and my parents seemed more interested in their own troubles than anything I was going through. It was bound to happen sooner or later; my mother finally left my dad. It happened in April of 1973, and I remember feeling that something was different the minute I walked into our house after school. I called out, "Mom!" but there was no answer. I called out louder for her and began to wonder where she could be. She never went anywhere except to news stand up the street to get cigarettes or a magazine, and that was usually in the morning. Just as I was ready to call out once more, the thought hit me that maybe she was sleeping. She would sometimes take a nap during the afternoon by lying on her stomach across the already-made bed. I quietly walked towards my parents' bedroom to check and see if she was in there sleeping, but when I got there and peeked inside, it was empty. At that point, the feeling that something was different grew even stronger and made me step inside the tiny little bedroom, where I almost immediately spotted a piece of paper on my mother's dresser. In two small steps I was quickly at the dresser; I picked up the piece of paper and began to read. My heart started beating faster and faster and it slowly sank in with each sentence I read. My mom was telling my dad that she didn't love him anymore and that she was leaving him.

A part of me must have been in disbelief, because I laid the letter back down and started checking her dresser drawers to see if any of her clothes were gone. As I opened and slammed each empty drawer, a feeling of panic overcame me. I then noticed that her wedding ring had also been laying there on the dresser. I immediately reached down and picked it up. For the first time, it finally hit me my mom was gone. I started crying uncontrollably, screaming, "No!" "No!" I didn't know where my mom was, or what to do, and I numbly walked out of the bedroom to the kitchen with the ring still in my hand. After looking down at it for awhile and crying the whole time, I just kept thinking, *What should I do?* Finally, after my crying subsided, I decided to call one of dad's sisters I was close to and tell her what happened. After telling her my mom had left, my aunt said she would call my dad and tell him.

After my mom left, it took quite awhile for things to settle down. I began to resent my mom. My dad had always portrayed himself as the good guy in my life and in my eyes, he could do no wrong. Since she was always made out to be the bad one in every argument they had, it made me assume it was her fault for leaving. Although I was devastated, I was also very angry, so I wanted to live with my dad. He would cry a lot after she left, and this made me feel very sad for him. I would feel even sadder for him after I heard a song on the radio that actually reminded me of my dad's situation. It was titled, "The Last Song," and after hearing it, I got the 45 r.p.m record of it so I could listen to it all the time. The one I am referring to now I haven't heard since that time, and I will write a few of the lyrics as I remember them today so you can understand why they touched me so dramatically back then.

Did you know I go to sleep and leave the lights on/
Hoping you'll come by and know that I was up and still awake/
This is hard for me to say/
but this is all that I can take.
Then the chorus would start
This is the last song I'll ever write for you/
It's the last time that I'll tell you just how much I really care/
But I love you/
Oh yes I do

Can you imagine being 13 years old, and feeling so sad for yourself and your father that you cried every time you heard that song?

Even with the impact everything had on me at this time, I still began seeing my mother a few weeks after she left, and by June, I would finish seventh grade. Summertime would officially start a couple of weeks later, but sadly, even as the weather changed and got warmer, nothing much changed with my dad. He was still miserable without my mother being there, and I was getting yelled at for every little thing. There were more than a few times, however, when I did actually deserve it. Like the time he went for the plastic gas can he used to fill up our lawnmower. After he found it missing, he got very angry and yelled at me about it disappearing. I lied and said I didn't know where it was, when in fact just a few days before I had burned it up in a fire. The incident started out by taking the plastic can along to a nearby trail, in case I needed to put more gas in the mini bike I owned. After me and my "tough guy" friend got to the trail and began to take turns riding it, on one of his turns, I got bored and started lighting weeds on fire with the matches I had for my cigarettes. Because I was running out of them, I decided to pour gas from the plastic can on the weeds to make them burn instead of using up more matches.

Unfortunately, I did this while the weeds were already burning, and as the flames got higher, they followed the gas trail to the plastic can and it also caught on fire. I got scared, quickly dropping the now burning container, and began kicking it in hopes of putting out the fire. The next thing I knew, the fire spread as more burning gas was spilling out everywhere from me kicking the can. Thank God the gas didn't get on me and the fire eventually burned itself out, or obviously the situation could have been much worse. The only part left from the gas can was the very bottom portion and there was no way I was going to tell my dad the truth. I knew he didn't believe me, but thankfully it was soon forgotten.

In early July, my mom finally took me to where she had been living. It was the home of a man she had dated before I was born and I'm certain on and off while dating my father. I also know my dad had a few different altercations with this man as a result of it, because he had actually told me about one of them. I felt very uncomfortable around this guy and didn't want to go there with her again. My dad didn't want me there either, especially now that the divorce was final, and I eventually didn't see my mom at all. She would call each week to say hello and tell me how much she missed me, but even though it was very hard not seeing her, I still stayed with my dad. I also continued hanging around with the tough guy and the pot dealer and some of their older friends from the neighborhood. For a short time they would all come to my house to hang out, but that ended when money disappeared from my dad's dresser; he blamed me, but would believe years later that I had nothing to do with it. I also got caught smoking by my dad when he came home unexpectedly and had to go to work with him for the next couple of days as punishment.

After that, things settled down and were actually uneventful the rest of the summer, until, of course, school started again. By lunchtime of my first day as an eighth grader, I would start a fight with another kid that my redneck friend would finish. I was standing in the lobby talking to him and a couple of other kids, and I told them I was going to start a fight with the next guy that walked by. I really didn't think it would come about, but when they spotted someone coming our way, they reminded me of my boast; without hesitation, I stepped in front of him and asked if he wanted to fight. He actually said yes, and even smiled as he looked down at me. After that we both agreed to go outside to fight, and other people began following us when they heard what was going to happen.

Once we finally reached an area behind the school where there weren't any teachers, we stopped and stared at each other, no one ready to throw the first punch. I think we both began to realize we didn't really want to take a chance of getting caught fighting, especially on the first day of school. (Actually I was afraid, because even though I knew he was bigger than me, I didn't realize how much bigger until we got outside.) We just stood there waiting for someone to either back down or throw the first punch, when my tough guy friend walked over and said, "I'll start it," and with that, hauled off and hit the other kid, who then retaliated. But because my friend was pretty big himself, it made for an even fight while it lasted. After only two or three minutes, a teacher came bolting out a door behind the school and broke it up, then took both of them to the office. I felt bad for my friend; he had been in fights the previous school year, and was probably in a lot of trouble, but I also thought I wasn't the one that involved him, and started to care less by the end of lunchtime.

However, shortly after lunch, I was called down to the office, and I got paddled for my part in the whole thing. Nothing happened to the other kid, which I guess was understandable, but unfortunately my tough guy friend got suspended from school. If only that would have been the end to both our troubles, but it wasn't. He eventually got expelled from school and I eventually started to use drugs other than marijuana. Before those drugs would become a part of my life though, my mother would again. A few days after the fight in school, she came back home, and I'll never forget my surprise. It was in the morning before school started, and my dad was at work. I was in the bathroom relaxing in a tub of hot water smoking a cigarette. All of the sudden the door opened and my mom walked in. I couldn't believe it was her, and don't recall if I felt embarrassed with her standing there just a few feet away because I was in shock. I do remember sitting up rather quickly though, but it was more to hide the cigarette by my side underwater than to hide myself. I don't know if she could tell if I was smoking or not, because she was only in there long enough to tell me to hurry up and get done, and it wasn't until she turned away and walked back out that she yelled, "I want you to go along and help me get clothes." As soon as I heard that, I sprang up out of the tub, dripping water everywhere, and flushed the wet soggy cigarette down the toilet. I knew this meant my mom was coming back home, and I got more and more excited as I quickly dried off and raced to my room to get dressed. I don't remember much else after that, except that we used a dark blue station wagon that belonged to the guy she had been staying with to go get her clothes and bring them back home. Other than that, I just remember we all lived happily ever after. Well, not exactly.

Although my mom and dad said they loved each other, and got married again for what was now their third time—once before I was born, again after their first divorce while I was still a baby, and the last time when I was thirteen with me as their witness)—they would eventually start fighting again. I would also start fighting in school again, and because I was the fearful and insecure thirteen-year-old who wanted so desperately to have friends in my life, I would also soon start using different drugs. I didn't really have any close friends, except a few different girlfriends at school, but since I never saw them outside of school, I didn't really get a chance to develop much of a relationship with them.

There was an older girl, though, that I lost my virginity to the very first time we met that I did at least try to get to know outside of school. However, after only the first date, I was too fearful and insecure to see her again. I remember we were at the mall together walking around when we ran into my tough guy friend, and in just a very a short time, I felt she was paying more attention to him than me. I already felt inferior around him, and her giving him any kind of attention only made it worse. That's why after that day, I just decided I wasn't good enough for this older girl and stopped seeing her. My parents surely wouldn't have noticed my low self-esteem. I never had the proper role modeling needed as I was growing up because of the constant bickering and fighting they displayed around me. All I ever got from my parents was them telling me they loved me, and toys, but it wasn't enough to compensate for the other things they didn't give me—the guidance and reassurance that I needed to grow emotionally, and to have a confidence in myself..

There is the normal type of pretending most boys do at five or six, like make believing you're a cowboy or a super hero, which I did. And then there was the other type of pretending I would do with my parents. I would pretend everything was all right between them after every fight they had until I finally started believing it. Of course, this would only last until the next fight, but it would make me feel better at the time and help me cope with my fears. It just evolved into me pretending to be something I wasn't as a teenager to make me feel better and so I didn't have to deal with my new fears and insecurities. Yet underneath all the bravado and acting out, there was still that scared little boy who just needed some reassurance that everything was going to be all right in my life, even though it wasn't.

When I was 14 years old and in eighth grade, I found a few new people to hang around with, and this is where I learned about the drugs called T and Mescaline. They came in a pill form, but were quite different. T was a low dose of something called phencyclidine, better known as PCP, and at one time was used as an anesthetic agent and animal tranquilizer. It was taken off the market because of its dangerous side effects, but in this low dose, it basically had an intoxication effect much like alcohol and would last several hours. I would spend a dollar to buy a "hit" from one of my "new friends" and take it before my first period class started. By the end of the class, I would stand up at the bell to leave, a rush would come over me, and I would begin to feel I didn't have a care in the world. Where marijuana had made me feel good, it wasn't as good as this, so I would take it many times more. On the other hand, I didn't like the way Mescaline made me feel. It came from a cactus called Peyote and was considered a psychedelic hallucinogen that could have effects similar to LSD, but not nearly as potent. Although some of my friends said they hallucinated while on it, I only felt anxious and sometimes paranoid.

On one such occasion, during lunch, I ended up in the school auditorium sitting in a circle smoking cigarettes with about ten other people. There were no lights on and all I could see when I looked around in the pitch black darkness was the ends of everyone's cigarettes glowing in the dark. I remember thinking the whole time that at any minute a teacher was going to come in and find us. Finally, near the end of the day, I came down from that high feeling tired and sad, and with little memory of all the day's events. I would stop taking Mescaline because of this, but would continue smoking pot, occasionally taking T, and trying to be something I wasn't. Eventually however, trying to be something I wasn't would help me stop smoking and taking drugs, and at fifteen years old, become a boxer.

3

Why I needed to be Something I Wasn't

Although I became a boxer at fifteen and stopped using drugs, I continued pretending to be something I wasn't because I needed so desperately to feel important. First it was by becoming a boxer, and later, chasing after girls and drinking. Once again when I needed guidance and reassurance, there would be no one for me to turn to except two people that would become my role models and I would try to emulate: Boxer Muhammad Ali, the Heavyweight Boxing Champion of the World, and the uncle that was like a brother to me when I was little. Now I realize there is a big contrast here, but make no mistake about it, they both played a big part in my behaviors as a teenager.

Muhammad Ali was not only famous and always the center of attention, but also very confident in himself. At this point in my life I wanted to be like that too. So much, in fact, that by the fall of 1975, I decided to take up boxing at a local gym and copy his style, which was dancing around and leaning away from your opponents' punches. I did realize though, that since I only weighed 115 pounds, I would never grow to be as big as him at 217 pounds. But I did dream of someday weighing 160 pounds and becoming the Middle Weight Champion of the World. I would also act like Ali in school by bragging and writing poems, and by throwing punches in the air to show everybody how fast I was. Dreaming of becoming a boxing champion some day and acting like Ali made me feel like I was someone important, and I quickly developed a big ego.

I learned that even a false sense of ego could help me pretend to be someone important, so I could at least temporarily overlook the fears and insecurities that I felt. I'd walk by myself through the crowded halls in school, watching all the other kids as they'd walk together laughing and talking with one another. I remember feeling left out, like I was in some foreign country and didn't know how to speak their language. Naturally I would try to talk to the other kids, but I simply didn't have the skills needed to carry on a serious conversation, and it seemed like the only place I felt comfortable talking was the classroom. At least there I could feel good about myself by making everyone laugh, including the teachers. That's why even though I was afraid to be a boxer, I would continue anyway because I was good at it and it made me feel good about myself.

By May of 1976, when I was sixteen, I won an Amateur Golden Gloves Championship and had my picture in the school and local newspapers. I think I may have even liked this feeling more than the ones that drugs used to give me. Like those feelings though, this one didn't last, because when school ended in June, so did the attention. All I had now was the memories of my former glory and little else, as the gym where I worked out closed for the summer. Like the summer before, though, I would at least get to hang around with my uncle again and have some fun. However, as far as my boxing career went, this turned out to be the wrong thing to do. By the time the gym finally opened back up in the fall, I was way out of shape, and when I didn't do so well while sparring against one of the bigger guys I had no trouble out-boxing in May, it immediately shook my confidence, and something in me changed. I remember after I got home from the gym that evening, going straight to my room and walking over to the dresser where I displayed my boxing trophies. As I stood there staring at them, tears came to my eyes, and I slowly began to take them down one by one and put them away. I was angry with what had happened to me while sparring earlier, and at that moment I decided if I couldn't be the best boxer in the gym, I would quit. My dream of being Middle Weight Champion was over, and I didn't know exactly what I was feeling, or what else to do except cry.

If I would have had some type of guidance and reassurance, I may have rethought my decision to quit, or at least understood what I was feeling, but I didn't. Like other times in my life, my parents, for whatever reason, didn't pick up on my emotions, and I would have to deal with them alone. My mother was actually glad I quit, as she hated me boxing in the first place, especially after my only loss. It was just my third fight and I was knocked out by someone I shouldn't have even been in the ring with. He was a nationally ranked boxer with over sixty fights, and this would be the last match she ever came too. My dad however, was proud that I boxed and enjoyed going to see all my fights, but I don't remember him saying much when I quit. This decision to quit boxing was something I regretted for a long time, and although I did have one more match when I was seventeen and won another trophy, I would never box again.

By that time, girls had become my new trophies, and another way for me to feel better about myself. Using girls to feed my ego had actually taken root the previous summer while hanging around with my uncle, and now that I had quit boxing, it wouldn't be long before it sprouted, and I would look towards him as my new role model. Not only was he around a lot when I was little, but he would be the first person I actually developed a real friendship with. It had started the summer before when I stayed with him and his wife a lot, and grew over the time I began boxing. As a matter of fact, he was there when I won the Golden Gloves, and knowing he was there played a part in my wanting to win so badly.

This influence over me would continue through the summer I spent with him after I won the Golden Gloves, and by the time I quit boxing in the fall of 1976, I had already started to act like him. Girls were attracted to him, he seemed very confident in himself, and at this point in my life, I wanted to be like that too. I was only sixteen and my uncle was twenty-four, which I believe was quite an age difference to be running around together. However, the fact that he was my dad's brother, and a decent person, played a part in why I was allowed to be with him, though it probably wasn't the best idea. Although he didn't do drugs or hang around with people who did, he did start drinking that summer, and so did I. Now we didn't drink all the time, and only did so in an attempt to be crazy and have fun. But there were a few times that we would get drunker than we actually wanted to, and I would initiate an argument that I'd be sorry for the next day. Of course, because we were like brothers, we also had arguments about stuff when we weren't drinking, which he always won. As a matter of fact, he won at everything we ever did together, like shooting pool, playing darts, and racing our cars in town. No matter how good a game I played, he played better, and though my 1969 Mach One Mustang was fast, his 1965 Corvette was faster. And so the pattern was set, that no matter what I did, he was better at it—except for boxing—especially when it came to talking with girls.

We would cruise through town in his Corvette on two different streets that ran parallel with each other known as "The Circuit." I would sit in the passenger seat and watch as he talked to different girls in other cars while driving beside them, and how they seemed to like him. This made me wish I could be like that too, and although Muhammad Ali was still my role model, it still influenced me enough to try and imitate my uncle as well. It began with him coaching me as I attempted to talk to girls while riding with him in his car, but eventually I would drive through town alone and nervously try my best to act like him. My pretty face and hot car made it easy to initiate some kind of conversation, and where it was hard for me to talk to the other kids in school just a few months before, I was now getting better at talking with girls. They would laugh at my jokes and seemed to like me, and this made me feel good about myself. This summer was also the one where I would meet a young girl at a pizza shop that my uncle and I went to. She worked there with her sister, and would become my first true love.

Although I hadn't developed a whole lot of confidence with girls yet, I still mustered up enough courage to ask her out, and she accepted. Sadly for her though, I would soon have the courage to ask other girls out while still dating her, and having sex with them too. On a few occasions, I would even break up with the pizza shop girl to see someone else, but because we loved each other, we would always get back together again.

In September 1976, as my eleventh grade school year was underway, I was still dating the pizza shop girl. I also still had the false sense of ego to help me overlook my fears and insecurities I felt, and would soon begin using it to pretend I was a ladies' man. Sadly, my cheating hadn't slowed down, and later that year, it all blew up when I met a younger girl in school who I was attracted to. After finding out she felt the same way, we quickly got to know each other and started going together. It was easy for me to see her and the pizza shop girl at the same time without either one knowing, but as my ego got bigger, they found out, and it ended up hurting the girl from school. After telling the pizza shop girl that someone in school liked me just to feed my ego and make her jealous, she put a suck mark on my neck so the girl from school would see it. Sadly, because it made me feel like a stud, I never once took into consideration how this young girl would feel after seeing it. I realize today, of course, how wrong this was, because I know she loved me, and this had to hurt her a lot back then. She moved away before school was over, and although we called each other a few times, we never dated again. For the rest of that school year, I remained faithful to the pizza shop girl until I finished eleventh grade in June of 1977. Then I got a job pumping gas and doing small jobs like oil changes at a garage where my uncle was a mechanic.

I soon started meeting girls that would come in for gas there and began cheating on the pizza shop girl with some of them. I would also officially start acting more like my uncle this summer, drinking a little more and running around town; I also met more girls to feed my ego. The end result was that I ended up hurting the pizza shop girl, as well as some of the other girls, by trying to be something I wasn't. Although I really thought it was ok to "play the field" when it came to girls, I needed to in order to feel better about myself. My final year in high school, I was still dating the girl I met at the pizza shop, and still working with my uncle at the garage. I could even get out of school early to work there because of a special class that was offered to seniors who had jobs. This was cool for me to be able to do this, because it set me aside from the other teenagers that didn't have jobs, and in my mind, to be envied.

Later that year, in November, I decided I wanted to try boxing one more time, and after only a few weeks of training, I won that last match I spoke of, and although winning it made me feel good about myself, by now girls were much more important for my ego than boxing was. All in all I really had it made at this time, and you would think it would be enough for me to feel happy and content, but it wouldn't. Later that school year, I turned eighteen, and I celebrated by getting drunk with my uncle and some of his friends at a popular bar in a nearby state where the legal drinking age was eighteen. This was fun and set the stage for me to be able to go there on my own whenever I couldn't find anyone to get beer for me.

One of those times was early in 1978, after my false sense of ego enabled me to finally ask out a girl from school. She was very cute and since she was also eighteen, we ended up driving to that nearby state with another couple to get a case of beer. By the time we got back, we were all pretty drunk. I decided we should all go to the house of a favorite aunt and uncle of mine where I would sometimes go to shoot darts so the girl from school could meet them. My real intention, however, was to show off the girl from school to impress my relatives, but after we got there, the plan quickly fell apart. First off, my uncle wasn't even there, and then the girl from school started getting sick from all the beer she had drank and threw up in my aunt's rec room. This night quickly came to end, and so did our dating after what happened a few days later. I went to her house to visit her and felt very shy and insecure around her. Because of these feelings, I decided that someone as pretty as her could never like someone as shy and skinny as me, and after that day, I was too afraid to ask her out again. I did at least ask her to sign my high school yearbook though, and she mentioned the time at my aunt's house, and ended with "Don't forget me." Out of all the people I knew who graduated with me that year, only six other girls had signed my yearbook.

Now you would think that winning the Golden Gloves and being as well known as I was in school, there would have been a lot more entries in my yearbook then just seven, but there's a very simple reason there wasn't. Even though some people probably did think I was a cool person, I simply didn't feel that way about myself. I had built my confidence on pretending to be someone I wasn't when all along I was actually an egomaniac with an inferiority complex, who in the last days of school was too afraid to ask anyone else but those seven girls to sign my yearbook. The ones that did sign it wrote some very nice things about me that included how much they enjoyed talking with me and that I brightened up their days with my humor, and one girl said she never met anyone like me. It not only made me feel good reading these things, but their words brought tears to my eyes as I realized each one of them knew the real Darryl and still liked him.

I can only wonder now if I'd had more help realizing back then that the real Darryl was good enough for people to like, maybe I wouldn't have tried as hard as I did to be someone important through high school and drink like I did. Or if I would have felt the need to continue drinking and acting like my uncle that following summer after I graduated. However, I am fairly certain that somewhere along the line, I would have eventually gotten drunk and liked it so much that I would have kept on drinking anyway. And I'm fairly certain that after meeting the beautiful blonde woman that would someday become my wife, my insecurities and low self-esteem would have eventually resurfaced and I would have started drinking even more. One thing I know with all the certainty in world is that just like what one of the girls who signed my yearbook also said, the woman who married me would indeed have her hands full.

4

Why I Got Married

If anyone would have asked me in September of 1978 what I wanted to do with my future, I couldn't have given them an answer. If someone would have asked me what type of person I thought I was at this time, however, I could have: I was someone who *liked* woman and beer, but *loved* his car. This would have also summed up my life at this time, as all I did was chase after girls, drink beer, and wash my 69 Mach One Mustang almost every day. I was eighteen years old and my parents weren't pushing me to move out or go to college, so I simply remained content working at the garage and getting drunk every Friday night. I was also still acting like my uncle, and using my false sense of ego to pretend to be a ladies man. It amazes me why girls were even attracted to me in the first place. I was thin as a rail, standing five foot eight inches and weighing only a hundred and twenty pounds. Being so skinny at my age only added to my feelings of insecurity, and no matter how much I tried to act like my uncle, I still felt that way inside. That's why I couldn't believe it when sometime in October, an older girl that I had a crush on in high school pulled into the garage where I worked and asked me out on a date.

I stood there beside her tan Volkswagen Beetle, smiling and feeling very shy as she introduced herself as the girl who had shared a class with me in school. She then asked me if I remembered her and although I did and acknowledged so, she looked entirely different than when I had a crush on her in 1976. At that time, she'd had straight, dirty blonde hair cut boyishly short, with a cute round face and a warm, friendly smile that I loved. Now she had long curly light blonde hair and looked like a model in a fashion magazine. She still had that same warm smile though, and it made all the old feelings I had for her flood back in. As we made small talk, all I could think about was how I couldn't believe it was really the same girl I liked so much in high school, and how beautiful she was.

Of course I tried to hide my nervousness by making jokes as we talked, but she seemed to like this and it made me feel good. A short time later however, this feeling would be replaced with disbelief, and then excitement when she asked me if I wanted to go out with her sometime. I had never before had anyone this beautiful even look my way, much less ask me out. But as excited as I was, my false sense of ego allowed me to remain calm as I replied, "Sure." We then exchanged phone numbers and said our goodbyes, and after she left, I immediately went inside the garage to tell my uncle what just happened. Although I still looked up to him, I had also become quite jealous of the fact that he was so popular with girls, and I wasn't. Now, however, someone more beautiful than any girl he ever knew had actually asked me out, and I couldn't wait to let him know. Our first date was in a bar, of course, and from then on, I was infatuated with her. Then, after only a few days of seeing each other, she would tell me she was falling in love with me, and I would tell her the same thing.

There was just one problem, though, and that was that the pizza shop girl was still a part of my life. Now you would think the simple solution to this would be to tell the pizza shop girl that, once again, I found someone new and wanted to break up, but I didn't. When it came time to do it, for some reason I couldn't, and I even ended up taking her to my uncle's house for Thanksgiving dinner. My future wife had already made plans to spend the holiday with her family, so it was easy for me to tell her I would just go by myself to my uncle's. Unfortunately, I also ended up taking the pizza shop girl to the garage later that same day so I could do something to my car, and was spotted by my future wife and her sister. They had gone to a convenience store across the street from the garage to buy cigarettes and saw me and the pizza shop girl leaving there in my car. She called me that night and told me to come to a beer distributor near her house to meet her, and bring along the pizza shop girl. I don't know why, but I agreed and took the pizza shop girl along, which of course turned out to be a bad move. They talked and agreed I was an asshole, then my future wife drove off angry and upset, and I drove off with the angry pizza shop girl. When I called my future wife the next day, she was still understandably angry and said she didn't want to ever see me again. I did my best to talk my way out of the situation, but it was no use, and I finally gave up after she told me we were through.

It hurt me that she didn't want to see me anymore, and as the days went by, I started to miss her so much that I called to tell her this, and admit that I was truly in love with her. She told me she felt the same way and eventually forgave me after I broke up with the pizza shop girl for the last time. By the following summer of 1979, my future wife and I moved in together. At first, it was neat playing house and living with a beautiful blonde like her, but little by little, as my drinking increased, so did the arguments—especially after we went to bars where we could get in easily without being asked for ID. Although I had initially enjoyed being seen in bars with my beautiful girlfriend, my fears and insecurities began to make me feel like I wasn't good enough for her. As this feeling grew and we started going out more, I would become jealous and angry if she talked to some guy she knew, or even if someone kept looking at her. Then depending on how much I had to drink, I would sometimes pick a fight with a random patron and cause a scene. Mostly though, it would be her that I would get angry toward and start a fight with, and no matter how much reassurance she gave me that she was mine and mine only, I didn't believe it.

Even getting married that year didn't help how I felt. She was pregnant and we needed my insurance to help cover the cost of having a baby. Sadly, I accused her that the baby wasn't mine. Eventually she convinced me it was, and insurance reasons aside, because I also loved her so much and would have eventually married her anyway, we made it official in November. After that, we spent our first Christmas together as a married couple in a small apartment we had moved into back in October. My wife had spotted it just up the street from where my parents lived and thought it was cute. It would also be practical, since my mother was going to watch the baby for us during the week while we worked. Unfortunately, this also would mark the beginning of where we would also argue about each other's parents. Although we both had a rough time with our respective in-laws, it was me who would start the arguments about how her parents were, and I would get mad if she said anything at all about mine. Of course, if it wasn't her parents, I would find something else to get mad at and argue over. In my warped mind, I never considered it was my fears and insecurities that were the problem, and finger pointing was becoming a way of life for me.

Sadly, so too was my drinking, and a pattern was forming where I would use these arguments as an excuse to get drunk. Although this pattern also included regrets and apologies the following day, it would continue and eventually increase. I don't fully understand, even today, how my wife put up with it all. The thought of that young, beautiful woman and the skinny, insecure nineteen-year-old being together just doesn't add up unless it was meant to be. Maybe she was supposed to see me that day at the garage, and maybe we were supposed to realize we wanted to be together. Maybe we were supposed to get married because she was supposed to get pregnant first. And maybe every damn thing I put that young innocent woman through at that time was meant to be, I don't know.

I do know that today I am so sorry for all of it, and wish I could go back in time to show her the kind of love she was looking for. I guess between the childhood I had, the awful teenage years I went through, and all the drinking I was doing, I never had a chance of giving her what she needed in her life until now. That's why I'm beginning to believe that maybe it was all meant to be, and that I was destined to be with my wife. It seems to be the only way I can explain why we stayed together this long, and especially in the beginning, other than the birth of my daughter in June of 1980. As much as I loved my wife, I can honestly say I loved my baby girl even more. I remember how happy I felt as I watched her being born, and how I cried with joy after the doctor laid her down on her mother's chest. I just stood there staring at this little miracle with awe and almost too afraid to touch her. Now you would think that because of the way I felt that day and the fact that I loved my wife so much, I would have been ready to settle down and learn to be a daddy, but you would have thought wrong.

After only a few months of trying to be a daddy and a good husband, something inside of me began to change and I began feeling afraid. I remember getting out of bed one morning to get ready to go to work, and as I was standing there between the bed and the crib in our tiny little bedroom that was part of our tiny little apartment, I looked to my right and stared down at my wife sleeping in our bed, and then to my left and stared at my little two-month-old daughter sleeping in her crib, and that's when it hit me. Not only was I married and had a baby, but I was going to a job that I never really wanted. I had taken it the previous year at my wife's insistence because it paid more than the one at the garage, and now with a baby, I needed it. Nevertheless, I was so scared that morning that I actually felt sick to my stomach, and I just wanted to pack up my clothes and leave. Thankfully though, I loved my wife and baby so much, I did what I thought a normal twenty-year-old man in my position would do. I went to work that day to support my family. Unfortunately though, when the weekends came, I did what an abnormal twenty-year-old with a drinking problem would do. I pretended everything was going to be all right, and ran away from my fears by drinking even more.

5

Why I Looked for Reasons to Run Away

When someone wants to drink like I did in 1981, they will find some of the silliest reasons to do so. It can be about dinner not being ready when they come home from work, or something even more ridiculous; like not having milk in the refrigerator. I should know because I used both of these reasons myself as an excuse to start a fight so I could go out to a bar, and of course, get drunk. Behind this "excuse finding," though, there was always an underlying reason why I wanted to drink, and it was always fear. I remember thinking how at this time, I was already tied down with a wife and baby, and had a job I didn't like. This not only made me feel afraid almost everyday, but to also worry about my future, be angry at times with my wife for getting pregnant in the first place, and feel so sad on some days that I pitied myself over all of this. I truly thought it was my circumstances that made me feel this way, and simply didn't realize that the fear was coming from all the insecurities I had about being a father and a husband, not to mention the fears I had about my job. Add in some occasional feelings of resentment along with my lack of coping skills, and you can begin to understand why I thought the best way to deal with my feelings was to simply run away and get drunk.

My wife, however, didn't understand all this at the time, and tried to slow down my drinking at home. I don't blame her, because she didn't like the way I acted when I got drunk, and certainly didn't want me around the baby when I was drinking. That's why after I turned twenty-one and could get into any bar legally, the "excuse finding" would begin so I could drink like I really wanted to with no limitations. Especially after we bought a house and money got tight. I remember feeling pushed into it by my wife, and having this added responsibility only increased my fears and insecurities. That's why by the end of 1981, although I couldn't see it, my drinking was getting out of control.

Sadly, this blindness that anything was wrong with how much I drank also prevented me from realizing that it was my fears and insecurities that made me want to drink, and I would go on believing it was my circumstances, like being in a job that I hated. It was working at a plumbing supply place, where I helped most of the customers with small jobs, and the bigger ones were handled by the owner's sons and other employees who knew much more about plumbing than I did . This made me feel inferior to everyone at work, and not even my false sense of ego could help me overlook that fact. I did, however, pretend I was a "Master Plumber" after I began working there in 1979 by doing simple plumbing jobs for a few of my relatives. But it stopped later in the year after I was faced with actually becoming one. I remember the idea of becoming a real plumber began shortly before I got married when my then future father-in-law told me he had talked to a friend of his who owned a big plumbing and heating business in our area. The owner told him that he would most likely hire me, and even give me on-the-job training. The day he took me there to simply fill out the application, however, my fears and insecurities kicked in big time, and after that day, I knew I didn't have the confidence needed to be a plumber. Instead I would remain at the plumbing supply place where I was now making more money than I did at the garage, and using my false sense of ego to pretend to be a big shot.

Naturally I was only acting this way to make me feel better about myself, but this behavior began affecting my relationship with my uncle, and we slowly drifted apart. Even sadder was the fact that I had begun missing him only a few months after leaving the garage, and by 1981, I wished I was still working there with him. I slowly built up resentment towards my job, and by the middle of the following year, I began hating it. I also began to build up resentment towards the owner's two sons that year. They were twins and only a year older than me, but would handle the customers with an ease I couldn't match and take on responsibilities with a confidence I didn't have. This made me jealous of them, and as I began drinking more, it only helped to magnify these jealousies and increase my resentment towards them and my job.

Eventually, as these feelings began to show and I started coming to work late and calling in sick a lot, it began to severely affect my relationship with them and their father, and they all simply grew tired of it. That's why, a few days after the New Year rolled in, their dad came up to me one morning and said he was laying me off because he didn't need me anymore. I really don't remember how I felt when he told me that, but I do remember I was hung over and very emotional at the time. I also remember asking him if I could collect unemployment, and him replying he didn't care. That's when my emotions got the best of me and I actually hugged him as a feeling of relief hit me. I was finally getting away from the job I hated and all the fears that I thought it caused, and I could even collect unemployment. As I said goodbye to him, I even thanked him, and walked to my car with tears in my eyes. I think a part of me realized, at that moment, that the owner really did care about me, and instead of firing me, laid me off so I could collect unemployment.

This emotion didn't last; however, as I began thinking how I was going to tell my wife I had lost my job, especially since we learned she was pregnant again only a month before. At first this made me feel scared, but I was so hung over from drinking the night before that all my thoughts quickly drifted towards just getting home and sleeping. That didn't happen right away, though, because after I got home and told my wife I had lost my job, she started crying and then began yelling as she questioned what we would do for money now with another baby on the way. I certainly didn't feel like arguing because of the hangover, and simply told her not to worry about it, that I would collect unemployment. Then, without saying another word, I went into our living room and lay down on the floor with some pillows to finally get some sleep.

The most awful part about that morning however, wasn't that I had lost my job, but that I had agreed to try and change after my wife had kicked me out of the house for two weeks only a few months before because of my drinking and the way I was behaving, and here I was now unemployed with her upset and crying, and all I wanted to do was go to sleep. It was this type of self-centeredness that often prevented me from caring how upset my wife got over my drinking or noticing how it affected our relationship and here it was rearing its ugly head again, but I couldn't see it. I also couldn't see this self-centeredness the summer before when all I did was get drunk as much as I could. It was that summer that actually led up to me being kicked out and was most likely the beginning of my alcoholic drinking. Summer was always a fun time for me. The sunny days without a cloud in the sky gave me an upbeat feeling and made me feel like celebrating by having fun. There were parties and cook-outs to go to, and they always added to my reasons to let loose and, of course, to get drunk. I also loved staying out late on some of the warm summer nights, and going bar hopping to find anyone else that wanted to have a good time.

Because of all of this, however, summertime wasn't all that fun for my wife, as she was either upset with me acting crazy at the parties and cook-outs, or home alone with our daughter on the nights I was out drinking. Unfortunately though, that summer in 1982 quickly became about me and me only, as I started to resent the fact that I had a job I hated, lived in a house I never wanted, and felt like I was trapped with a wife and child. Me, me, me is all I thought about as I would first make myself angry about my circumstances and then begin to pity myself over them.

Having these emotions actually gave me a comfortable feeling that I liked, because I was used to feeling this way, and because I knew they would almost always lead to the same conclusion: starting a fight with my wife and then believing I had enough justification to go out drinking. I still remember how I would hold onto these emotions while actually out at a bar, but only long enough to further justify drinking, and then I'd move on to the emotions I was really looking for—the ones that made me feel like I didn't have a care in the world, and everything was going to be all right. I did this by drinking my first three or four beers as quickly as I could to get the warm buzz I liked so much, and then I would slow down slightly, and push the thoughts of my job and having a wife and baby completely out of my mind. Then I wouldn't stop drinking until I was out of my mind as well.

It didn't matter if it was during the week or the weekend. If I was out and started drinking, although I felt deep inside that I should be home with my family, I wouldn't stop drinking and go home. "To hell with everything" was my motto when I wanted to get drunk, and nothing was going to stop me. Darryl was the center of the universe that whole summer, as my false sense of ego now helped me to be the crazy drunk who just wanted to have fun. Never once did I consider my wife's feelings or the consequences of my actions leading up to one of my drinking sprees, but only after, and the next day was always the same. While full of remorse, I would tell my wife how sorry I was and promise to slow down on my drinking, or depending on how mad she was, I would even quit drinking for a awhile and try to behave the way she wanted me to—loving and caring. Slowly but surely, however, I would start finding reasons why I wasn't happy, like my wife didn't love me or that she just didn't understand me, and then use it as an excuse to get drunk. I never thought about how much she wanted me there with her and our daughter on those summer nights or realized how lonely she was. I just wanted to run away from the fears I had and never realized that she had them too.

Finally, by that October, after the promises to stop drinking became less frequent and staying out late was happening more, my wife told me she was fed up with my drinking and my behaviors and thought we should separate for awhile. Even after she told me this, I still couldn't understand why she was so upset, and right away I made it about me by yelling out that this proved she never truly loved me. I then started crying as I realized that she really meant it when she said she wanted to separate and when my pleading for us to stay together failed to change her mind, a fear like I never experienced before came over me. For some reason, though, I didn't drink that night and when the morning came, I went to work and cried some more while telling my boss what happened. He must have known I couldn't work that day as upset as I was because he gave me the day off, and after I got back home I began feeling even more upset as two frightening thoughts came to mind. What would I do if my wife and I didn't get back together? And how would I be able to handle not seeing my daughter everyday? Then as I kept thinking about the whole situation, the worry slowly turned to anger as I started wondering why my wife couldn't see the good qualities in me. I understood how my drinking and staying out late some nights might upset her, but why couldn't she see what a good husband I really was? I paid the bills and spent time with her when we did things with our friends. And why couldn't she remember the days when I was being her "Old Darryl" and acting loving and caring towards her? And couldn't she see that I loved my daughter more than life itself?

The problem, however, wasn't what I thought my wife couldn't see, but that I couldn't see how my self-centered fears, insecurities, and negative emotions of worry, anger, sadness, and self pity were to blame for my drinking and my behaviors, and that I was the problem, not everything else in life. I couldn't see that paying the bills didn't make someone a good husband, but was just one of the many responsibilities of being one. And I couldn't see that my wife needed me there with her for companionship and help with the baby, and not just when we were with friends. I couldn't see how simply loving my daughter and holding her now and then wasn't enough to call myself a father. And I also couldn't see how verbally abusive I was towards my wife sometimes and how neglected she and my daughter really were. I had talked myself into believing all the excuses I made for my drinking, and a week later I couldn't even understand why I was being kicked out of my house by my wife and felt resentful that I would have to move back in with my mom and dad. I used the separation as an excuse to continue drinking, but in reality I knew no other way to handle the situation, and neither did my mom or dad, so I couldn't look to them for any guidance.

The only other thing besides drinking that I felt I could do at the time to help me deal with my situation was something I would deeply regret. I would turn to another woman for some kind of solace, who my wife knew and disliked at the time: The Pizza Shop Girl. I'm not proud of this choice and can only say that I was truly a different person back then, and that my actions were spawned by my fears and insecurities, and by believing the excuses I made for drinking. I was just so angry and resentful at my wife for kicking me out, and so scared to be alone, that I just wanted company. I'm surely not condoning anyone having an affair, and will add here that it was actually me who often accused my wife of having affairs. Once again this was due to the blindness I had to the fact that anything was wrong with me, and that I was the problem, not another man. I didn't seem to remember all the times she pleaded with me to stay home with her and told me how tired she was of being alone. Or all the times she would tell me how much she loved me, and just wanted her old Darryl back. And I didn't remember all the times she told me she just wished I would stop drinking for good. I wish that I would have listened to her. I also know she was right in kicking me out back then because of the way I was treating her. What I don't know is what possessed her to let me move back in after only two weeks of being apart. Maybe it was because she missed me and still loved me. Or maybe it was because she was pregnant and scared with no place to go; you can take your pick. Which is what I did shortly after we got back together, and you know what my pick was? I decided she only got back together with me because she was pregnant and had nowhere to go, and guess what? I had another excuse to keep on drinking.

I was drinking the night we got back together and you already know I was drinking the night before I lost my job in January of 1983. I also drank the night my son was born that following August, and continued to drink on and off through the rest of that year. I even drank the night before I left for Boot Camp on February 3rd, 1984, but remember thinking I would stop now that I was going into the Army. I believed that the Army would help straighten me out, and my life would change for the better. My wife and I had already sold our home the summer before and moved into a smaller, less expensive apartment to help with the finances, plus I would get a small bonus for enlisting in the Reserves. My wife also believed that by me joining the Army I would finally quit drinking for good, and when I got out we could truly be a happy family. I even envisioned getting into great shape while in basic training and maybe even boxing again when I got out. My false sense of ego was running full steam ahead around this time, and I soon became the hero going away to the Army to support my family.

As a matter of fact, I wasn't the least bit frightened the morning I left. My wife however, was sad and upset that morning as she hugged and kissed me goodbye, and then began crying. I told her I would write her and try to call her as soon as I could, and that everything was going to be all right. Two days later, however, it was me that was crying as I lay on a bunk in a building the Army called the Processing Center, while writing my first letter home. In it, I told my wife how much I missed her, and that I loved her more than ever. I also wrote a poem for her on the other side of it, and still have it today, along with all the other letters we sent each other while I was in the Army. Every one was pretty much the same, as I would write how great things would be when I got home, how much I loved her and the kids, and how I missed them all so very badly. I was so glad the time went quickly while in basic training because realizing all of this made me feel sad and very homesick.

My basic training was in South Carolina, which for me was a very long way from home, and only added to my feelings of sadness. Finally, after two and a half months, I graduated from basic training, and in April went to Virginia for Advanced Individual Training. This was not only closer to home, but much easier than Basic Training, and seemed more like being at a college than in the Army. It was for this reason that I think I finally broke down one night and got a little drunk at a bar on base. I had actually had two beers at a bowling alley a week before, but this time, because I'd had too much to drink, it caused a small argument with my wife. Although I was drunk, instead of lifting my spirits, it made me feel even sadder, and after leaving the bar I decided I just had to talk to her. Only a few minutes into our phone call though, she asked me if I had been drinking, which made me very angry, and I snapped at her for asking. The real reason for this was that I was actually mad at myself for getting drunk and in my mind, letting her down. Although I quickly apologized for snapping at her, instead of telling her the truth as to why I got so angry, I lied and said I hadn't been drinking.

Of course, the next day I felt bad about the whole thing, and the slight but nagging hangover I had made me feel worse. It was soon forgotten, however, and after a few more weeks I was able to graduate from my Advanced Training and could finally go home and be with her and the kids. It felt good being home with them, and after quickly getting a good job as a machine operator at a local potato chip factory, everything was in place for us to be a happy family. After only a few weeks, though, I started working second shift, and my hours changed to three o'clock in the afternoon until eleven at night. My wife would wait up for me, but we still couldn't spend a lot of time together except on the weekends. I also only saw the kids in the morning, when I would watch them until my wife got home from working at her mother and father's hair salon where she worked as a hairdresser. But it still wasn't the same as being with them in the evenings when my wife was home. Also, the mornings simply seemed to go by too fast, and after lunch I would have to start getting ready for work so I could be there before my shift started. I began hating my job, and I didn't want to work there anymore. Fortunately, a break came my way in August when my wife told me that one of the neighbors had recently opened up a small home improvement company and was interested in hiring me as a salesman. She had become friends with him and his wife, and told them about me and my job situation.

I didn't waste any time as I went over to their house that weekend and introduced myself. Within a short time, he told me he liked my outgoing personality and the way I loved to talk, and added that he felt I would make a good salesman for his company. That was all I needed to hear to accept the job. As I stood there on his back porch looking over the window sample he had shown me earlier, I took another sip of the beer he had offered me and began feeling excited about my new job. After all, I was soon going to be the best salesman anyone ever met.

6

Why I Needed an Ego More Than a Family

One definition of ego is a person's sense of self-esteem or self-importance, and I think having this kind of ego can help a salesperson be successful in their job. However, another definition for ego, which is an exaggerated sense of self-importance, was closer to the kind I needed to have to be successful in mine. It's true that with some training and a few months of sales under my belt, I did become a very good salesman. It's also true that by the summer of 1985, my false sense of ego was in full swing as I began acting like I knew all there was to know about selling. I was either boasting about all the sales I had written for the company or critiquing some of the other salesmen to help them improve their selling abilities. I would also act like a tough guy by talking about my boxing days, or telling embellished stories of barroom fights I got into. Other times, I was the funny guy who thought he could make anyone laugh. I also started going out and getting drunk instead of only drinking at home on the weekends. As the year progressed, I began to spend less and less time with my family. This was only the beginning, though, as during the following year, I began to run around with a new salesman at work who also liked to go out and get drunk.

He had been a top salesman at a much larger company than this one, and even though his ego rivaled mine, we seemed to click the first time we met and immediately started drinking together. After becoming close friends over that year, he would reveal his ambitions to me of starting his own home improvement business, and by 1987, we would become partners in a small window and siding company. It was precisely because of our drinking and our egos. however, that only two and a half years later, the business would close and in January of 1990, I would actually give sobriety a try.

Back after I got out of the Army, I started needing an ego more than a family. When I first came home, I definitely needed to be with my family more than anything else—I realized how much my family truly meant to me when I was at basic training. Then, after I got out and took the job at the potato chip factory, the hours I worked prevented me from being with my family as much as I wanted to. This kept me in a state of longing for them, and I would begin to feel very sad when I had to leave for work. This sadness would continue after I got there because of the insecurities I felt about being a machine operator. The other machine operators were very good at keeping the potato chip machines running smoothly, but I wasn't and frequently needed their help. I also felt nervous and shy around everyone who worked there and tried to compensate for that by joking around and being friendly; I was later told by a nice woman that I became friends with that a lot of people didn't like me because of this behavior and the fact that I was new there. This hurt my feelings and added to the insecurities I already felt, and for the first time I can remember, I didn't use my false sense of ego to help me feel better.

Between the longing I had to be with my family and all my fears and insecurities, only a real sense of ego could have helped me feel better, and so instead of trying to be something I wasn't or going out and getting drunk, all I felt I could do was hope everything would be all right. Fortunately, it wasn't long after this that I accepted the job at the home improvement company and happily quit the potato chip factory. Over the next two weeks, I would go through training at the home improvement company, and although I had fears and insecurities about being a salesman, it wouldn't take me long to sell my first deal. As the rest of 1984 went by, I continued to make sales, and although I was spending time with my family, I also continued to drink on the weekends. The following year, though, as the company started to hire more salesmen and I started to worry about being the best one there, it didn't take long for my false sense of ego to return and by that summer, my drinking would once again start coming before my family.

When I was drunk, I could completely forget about everything, and be the kind of person I wanted to be—a hot shot salesman and tough guy who had a sense of humor that everyone liked and was the kind of guy every woman wanted. Although my "false sense of ego" allowed me to keep up this act when I wasn't drinking, without the alcohol to help me believe it, I often felt miserable as the fears and insecurities I felt would get the best of me and bring my negative emotions to the surface. I was always worried about not being the top salesman and would get jealous and angry when someone sold more deals than I did. Or I was worried that my wife didn't love me as much as I loved her, and I would get mad whenever I thought she wasn't showing me enough affection. I was also often sad for one reason or another, which I'm sure at times, was actually depression. And finally I'd get the "poor me" feelings so bad that it often led to self-pity.

This downward spiral continued through 1985, and by the following year, it seemed the only time I really felt happy was when I was out drinking, which I began to do a lot more of after meeting the salesman I would go into business with. Of course, there were periods when I would quit for awhile, like I had in the past, in an effort to be a family man. However, also like in the past, sooner or later the urge to drink would return and my drinking would once again come before my family. It would also come before the business I started with the salesman in 1987 and over the next two and a half years as my drinking continued to come first, the consequences began to catch up with me. First in November of 1989. After my partner and I had yet another argument over something stupid while drinking, we decided it was best to end our partnership and our friendship. Then at the start of 1990 after I came home drunk one night and started yet another fight with my wife, she told me she was leaving me if I didn't stop drinking. So with my business officially ending that month and the threat of my wife leaving me fresh in my mind, I knew it was time to attempt sobriety.

The only way I knew how to stop drinking though was to ask a former drinking buddy for help. I knew he had been sober for awhile. He had actually taken me to an AA meeting a few years before after another of my wife's threats to leave me, but that same night, I decided I wasn't an alcoholic and never went back. Now he was telling me there was a great possibility I was, in fact, an alcoholic and if I wanted him to, he would help me to try and stay sober. Because I now knew I had a drinking problem, I accepted his offer and started going to AA meetings, but the decision had much more to do with the fear I was feeling at this time. Not only was I afraid my wife would really leave me if I didn't stop drinking, but I was also worried about my finances. Although I had saved up enough money to live on for several months, without any income, I decided it was best to sell the new cars my wife and I drove and buy older ones that didn't have monthly payments. I also began looking for a new job, but because it was hard for me to accept the fact that I would now have to work for someone else, I stopped looking after a short time and decided to work on staying sober first. As worried as I was around this time, a part of me still felt relieved that I no longer had a business. I didn't have the fears and responsibilities associated with owning a business, but also I could now stop acting like "Mr. Big Shot Business Owner" I had been pretending to be.

After only a few months of going to Alcoholics Anonymous, I would begin a new act and become "The Know-It-All-Alcoholic." I would do this by telling everyone what they needed to do in order to stay sober and often quote word for word from books written to help alcoholics and the AA literature just to sound impressive. Doing this and acting like "The Know-It-All-Alcoholic" made me feel like I was important, and I would go to as many meetings as I could to continue to feel that way. However, as time went by and my savings started to run out, I started to feel fearful again, and with the prospect of having to go out and find a job close at hand, my false sense of ego was soon able to persuade me that I wasn't an alcoholic. Instead of taking an honest look at myself and truly trying to practice the Twelve Steps, all I had done over the eight months I was sober was go to meetings and pretend to be something I wasn't. When my fears began to overwhelm me, the only way I knew how to handle them was to use my false sense of ego to overlook them and tell me I could drink again. That day I called my wife and told her that I was planning on going to a bar and only drinking a beer or two to prove to myself I wasn't an alcoholic, and when I hung up the phone I drove to a nearby bar and indeed only drank two beers that day.

As a matter of fact, I would continue to limit my drinking, and even after I took the job as a salesman for a window and siding company in September, I would only stop in a bar after a sale to drink a few beers and then go right home. I know my wife still didn't like me drinking, but it pleased her that it seemed to be under control and that I was coming home early. On the other hand, drinking like this wasn't pleasing me, and by the following year I started to drink a little more. However, because I was still able to maintain control, my wife remained fairly happy throughout that year, and even when the company I had been working for went out of business, we didn't let it ruin our Christmas.

All in all, 1991 had been a good year for us as a family even considering I was drinking again, and after taking yet another new job in January of 1992, things would continue to go well. Once again, this was a home improvement company, but this one also sold insulation for the attic and walls of homes to improve a home's energy efficiency. I got the job because I knew someone there that I went to high school with and when I found out he remembered my reputation as a boxer, it was easy for me to start pretending to be "The Tough Guy" soon after starting there. After this it didn't take long for my false sense of ego to start growing bigger and by the spring of that year, he and I would leave there and open up a business of our own. As it turned out, although he wasn't a drinker, he had more problems than I did and I would end up owning the business myself a short time later. I did all right by myself the rest of that year, but by March of 1993 I was barely making enough money to pay my bills. As afraid as I was during this, though, I still maintained some control over my drinking, but it was slowly becoming harder to do. In April, I only sold enough jobs to pay my bills for maybe two more months and as May went by without even a prospect of a sale happening, I didn't know what I was going to do and soon became filled with fear and desperation.

I tried to fight these feelings, but near the end of the month, one day I became so overwhelmed by them that I got down on my knees and prayed to God to help me. Although I wouldn't realize it until a few weeks later, that weekend this prayer would be answered. On Saturday, my wife and I went to visit a couple we had become good friends with and who I liked to drink with, and after some beers and conversation, the wife asked me how business was going. I told her it wasn't doing very well and that I was worried, but I didn't say anything about praying earlier that week. She said she was sorry to hear this and asked me what I was going to do. I told her I wasn't sure, but hopefully I would find a job so I could close down my business. She then asked me what I thought about working as a salesman at an electronics and appliance store she and her husband had purchased a few things from. I told her I didn't really know anything about electronics or appliances sales, but that I guess I could at least stop in and talk to someone about a job there. The conversation soon switched topics and as the night went on and I kept drinking, my worries quickly disappeared.

That following week, I went to the store she had told me about and after looking around and talking to some of the salespeople, my false sense of ego told me I would have no problem being the number one salesman there. As it turned out, they needed an additional salesman for the electronics department and a few days later, I had an interview with the assistant manager who took an immediate liking to me. We started the paperwork, and a week later after a second interview with the store manager, I was officially hired. I would receive some training for the first two weeks, and by the end of that summer I was doing quite well selling the different brands of electronics and the extended warranties we were supposed to push. It made me feel good about myself to be working there and making a lot of money, and it felt good to know that God had apparently helped me. However, soon I would start to feed my ego by feeling important, and as much as I loved my family and wanted to be with them, my drinking would once again start coming first. I would try many times over the next few years to stop drinking, but the urge to drink kept coming back sooner after each time I quit. It would take that morning in 1996 to make me realize I had to finally stop.

7

Why I Finally Felt I had to stop Drinking

"Once the seed has been planted that someone's an alcoholic, that person's drinking can never be the same." It states something to this effect in the AA literature, and I can tell you after going to AA for all those months, there was definitely something different about my drinking afterwards, and over the next five years it became more and more evident. Although I would still pretend to be someone important, my drinking wasn't allowing me to believe it like in all the years before, and even when I was drunk, I knew I wasn't who I pretended to be. I also began to feel guilty about being out in bars drinking instead of being home with my family. My conscience started to kick in now even after my first few beers in a way it hadn't before, and I knew I would wake the next morning filled with regrets. Sadly, this still wouldn't make me stop, and I'd eventually push those feelings aside and continue drinking until I was drunk. Nevertheless, because the seed had been planted that I may be an alcoholic, over time, along with my conscience, it would lead to the morning I knew I simply couldn't go on living that way.

That was why I went back to AA for help, and would recommend it to anyone who thinks they may be an alcoholic, or even if they have a drinking problem. Although I feel it's not for me to call anyone but myself an alcoholic, and understand it can be a very strong word for a lot of people who drink, I still believe there are many drinkers out there who would benefit greatly by going to AA. One thing's for sure, whether you're an alcoholic or simply drink too much; I doubt that you're happy.

I've encountered different types of drinkers over my lifetime. Only you will know if you're one of these types, but remember, it doesn't mean you're an alcoholic. The only thing I ask of you is to ask yourself, "Are you truly happy?" First, I've seen the "'Agrees To Have a Beer When Asked' Drinker." He often replies with, "Sure, what the heck, I'll have one," and for the most part that's all he drinks. He seems to enjoy life and appears to be happy. Then there is the "'Two Drink' Drinker". Although he or she may talk about letting loose and getting drunk at some occasion, when the time comes, that person only has two drinks and then stops. Usually this is because these people don't like the way they feel after the buzz hits them on only their second drink. My wife is this type of drinker, and is normally a happy person.

Another type of drinker I've seen is the "Social Drinker." These people mostly have only a few drinks at parties or gatherings where alcohol is served, but there are times when they may drink more and get a little drunk. For the most part they appear to be happy, although some can be a little obnoxious, and even rude. Then there's the "Binge Drinker." Some of these types of drinkers have been in the news because they have actually died from alcohol poisoning and are usually college students. Sadly, some of these people may have been happy with their lives, but got caught up in the peer pressure that has become more evident on college campuses, where drinking to extremes is considered by some students to be normal. Although by binging, they were definitely abusing alcohol at the time, a lot of them still weren't the next type of drinker—"The Abusive Drinker." Although they may show control sometimes at parties where there is alcohol by either not drinking or limiting how much they do drink, these people rarely show control when they're in the mood to let loose and simply drink to get drunk. Usually, I find they have done this type of "partying" almost all their lives and don't really enjoy any other way of drinking. I also find they like the feeling that being drunk gives them, and although they may function quite well when sober, and be very decent people, many of them seem to have an all-or-nothing attitude that can sometimes cause them to be unhappy in their lives.

Finally, there is the "Problem Drinker." This particular type of drinker is almost always someone you either know or have heard about. It can be a friend of a friend, or someone in your own family. It usually confuses the people close to the "Problem Drinker" that even when this person realizes that all the trouble they get into is because of their drinking, they still won't stop. They may even admit they know they have a drinking problem and tell you how they hate themselves and aren't happy, but will still get drunk because their fears are too much for them to handle. Out of all the types of drinkers I mentioned, I can certainly relate to the "Problem Drinker" more than any other. Like this type of drinker, I also hated myself and wasn't happy, and it was my fears that usually got me drunk too. Even after I stopped drinking, I still didn't like myself and needed to use The Twelve Steps of Alcoholics Anonymous to help me understand my fears so I could begin facing them and become a happier person. This was completely different to what I had done most of my life, which was to pretend to be something I wasn't to try and overlook my fears in an attempt to be happy.

When I was a small child, I pretended to be a secret agent, or Superman, but that was just a part of growing up. Unfortunately, I also had to start pretending everything was all right between my parents when I was growing up to help me relieve the uncertainty and fear I felt every time they argued. As I became a teenager, though, this quickly evolved into me pretending to be something I wasn't in order to overlook the fears and insecurities I had developed through my childhood so I could feel better about myself and be happy. After that I tried to act like other people to feel good about myself and developed a "false sense of ego" to help me pretend to be important. Finally, I would use alcohol to believe I was whatever I pretended to be, and years before I realized it, became an alcoholic. The type is known in AA as a High Bottom Alcoholic. This is someone who still has their health, their family, and their job, but whose life has become unmanageable. The same type of people, although they're not alcoholics, still use alcohol, or anything else they can, to help them try to be happy. It can be drugs, sex, gambling, or even their jobs, but what they really need to do is learn how to love themselves enough to be happy with who they are.

I know because I was never happy in my life, and didn't even like myself until I began trying to become a better person. Not better than other people, but better than I was before. When we try to be better people, it helps us to like ourselves and be happy. But more importantly, it helps us to grow spiritually, which then enables us to love ourselves enough to eventually become happy with who we are.

8

Why Spiritual Growth enabled me to Love Myself

I didn't start trying to be a better person than I was before until after I began believing three things. One, that when people at AA meetings said they were happier now sober than at any other time in their life, they were telling the truth. Two, that the statement in the AA literature, "The same person will drink again," was very much a fact of life for most alcoholics. And three, that taking the Third Step of Alcoholics Anonymous was the key to me becoming a different person so I wouldn't drink again, and someday be happy. I had already taken the First Step, where I learned the difference between myself and what AA called a "Low Bottom" Alcoholic. And I had done the Second Step, which basically told me that we must realize we have not been sane when it came to our drinking, and no matter what our beliefs about God are, this step is the rallying point that can restore us to sanity.

   It wasn't until after I finally took the Third Step that I realized I would need to believe in what all of the steps told me, and constantly practice the rest of them as a way of life, if I wanted to change as a person and remain sober and happy. What I didn't realize at the time was that this step had also put me on the path of spiritual growth that would someday enable me to love myself and be happy with who I was. Although I am not permitted to write these steps as they appear in AA literature, here in my own words are the steps I took that helped me to grow spiritually by trying to be a better person than I was before. One. Acknowledged I couldn't handle alcohol, and that my life was no longer manageable. Two. Slowly began to believe that a Power greater than myself could help me become sane. Three. Decided to turn my will and my life over to the care of whatever God I understood there to be. Step Four. Without fear, took a searching moral inventory of myself. Step Five. Acknowledged to God, to myself and to another person the nature of my wrongs. Six. Were completely ready to have God take away all my character defects. Seven. Humbly asked this God to remove my flaws. Eight. Made a list of any people I had harmed, and became willing to make reparations to them. Nine. Made reparations to these people if possible, except when it would hurt them or others. Ten. Continued to fearlessly take an inventory of myself and when wrong admitted it right away. Eleven. With prayer and meditation tried to improve my conscious connection with whatever God I understood there to be, praying only to know what its will was for me and the strength to do it. And Twelve. Having been awakened spiritually by doing these steps, I tried to share this experience with alcoholics, and to practice what I had learned in my everyday life.

Sounds like a lot, I know, and believe me, there were times early on in my sobriety when I thought about giving up and drinking again, but practicing these steps as best I could helped me get through those times. There was one moment, however, when after being sober just a few months, I did come within seconds of saying, "The hell with everything!" and indeed getting drunk. The day had gotten off to a rocky start when an argument between me and my wife began that morning about something I no longer remember. I just know that I had recently changed jobs and even though I was trying my best to practice the Twelve Steps, I'd fall back to my old ways when the fears and insecurities I felt there sprung up, and sometimes I'd take it out on her. Anyway, I thought I better go to an AA meeting as soon as I could because of how angry I felt afterwards, and since I was off work that day, I decided to go to the noon meeting I sometimes attended. I don't remember too much about the actual meeting, though, except that when it was over, I was still mad and didn't feel any better. Normally, I would at least feel a little better after one, but this time I was simply too wrapped up in my thoughts of anger and self-pity to bother listening to anything positive that was shared there that day.

This must have shown, because as I was about to leave, another alcoholic that I knew from the meeting came up to me and asked how I was doing. At first I didn't want to tell him about the argument I'd had with my wife and how I was feeling because of it, but something about him encouraged me to open up and talk to him anyway. After awhile, he asked me if I wanted to stop by a halfway house where he and some other alcoholics got together for lunch to talk some more. I didn't really want to because I was still very nervous around people I didn't know, but he was able to persuade me to meet him there and gave me directions. As I drove there, I began to feel nervous and was getting even angrier at my wife about the argument we had. On top of that, I couldn't find the halfway house and began to feel frustrated. The directions were simple enough, but I just couldn't find the address my friend had given me. I remembered he had told me that when I saw the address on the front of the building to go to the next street and turn left, then take another left off of that street into an alley that would lead me around to the back of the building where there was a parking lot.

When I finally did find the address he gave me, for some reason I had trouble determining which place it was after driving around back, and by the third attempt, I stopped my car in the alley, put it in park, and sat there angry and filled with frustration. All I could think about was how this and everything else that day was reason enough for me to say, "The hell with everything" and go get drunk, until for some reason I looked over to my left and realized I was actually parked behind the halfway house I was trying to find the whole time. It was at this same moment I remembered something I had read previously in the AA literature. "There will come a time in every alcoholic's sobriety when the only thing that can come between him and his next drink is believing in a Higher Power." From that day on, there were still a few more times when I felt like giving up, but the urge to drink was never again as strong. I believe that this day was needed for me to come to believe that there is guidance from something I call God if we look for it, and that this experience was needed in my first year of sobriety for me to grow more spiritual. The rest of that first year went much better, and I soon began what is known in AA as the Pink Cloud Stage, where everything just seems good.

As a matter of fact, by 1997, I was feeling so good that I decided although my first anniversary of being sober wasn't until April, I would treat myself and my wife to a boxing event held in March in Atlantic City. It was for a boxing magazine's 75th anniversary of being in publication and many famous retired boxers were there. Still a big fight fan at this time, it thrilled me to no end seeing these fighters, and even though I was 37 years old, I felt more like an excited teenager when I'd walk up to meet them. I also felt like a teenager in other ways too, because it would take me awhile to build up the courage to do it, and when I finally did, I was very nervous around them. Much of this was due to only being sober for such a short amount of time and still having insecurities, but this event was still a lot of fun for me, and I know my wife really enjoyed it too. We would also enjoy a vacation that June with our children and other than some anxiety, as it would be the first one I'd had sober, it went very well.

This would contrast greatly, however, to the experience I would have at an event we all attended together in July. This one was in Pittsburgh at the Light Amphitheater where we went to see some bands play at The Warped Tour; we went because our daughter was singing there in a band. We left very early in the morning to go to Pittsburgh, and when we got there, everyone was tired. Everyone included my wife, my daughter, a friend of hers, and my son. We met the rest of the band and the man who managed them at the Light Amphitheater. It took some time to figure out where they should set up to play, and what time they would go on, but eventually everything was in place for them to perform that day. There was a lot going on at this event, and it was very hectic for everyone for awhile. Finally, after getting something to eat, my wife and I decided to find a motel to stay at for the night and try to get some rest before it was time for our daughter to sing.

We felt it safe to leave our thirteen-year-old son at the event in the care of our seventeen-year-old daughter and the manager we knew well, but after we found a motel and finally settled down, it didn't take long before we began to worry about leaving our son there, so we left to go back. We got lost and had to ask for directions, but eventually we found it along with our son and everyone else. Finally the band got its turn to perform, and although my wife and I enjoyed listening to our daughter sing that night, we were still glad when it was over. After returning to the hotel and settling down, we all watched a movie together before going to sleep.

At this time in my sobriety, I had replaced the obsession to drink with the obsession to stay in shape by running and lifting weights. After I woke up early that next morning, still tired from the day before and feeling quite miserable, I still thought it necessary to go workout in the small fitness area provided by our motel. I came close to calling it off, but then decided I just had to make up for not working out the day before. I didn't even have breakfast yet, which I should have. I lifted weights for a short period, and then got on a treadmill to run. I had never been on one before, and wasn't sure how to set it up properly. I simply hit a few different buttons to make it start going and set the speed to what I felt was a comfortable pace. I must of have pushed a wrong button, however, because it would periodically raise up in the front to simulate running up a hill, and at times go faster than the pace I had originally set. Imagine me now on this treadmill trying to run for two miles, and all the while it keeps getting faster, and rising up in the front making it even harder to run. Even though I was feeling even more tired than before from lifting weights, I was still determined to stay the course until those two miles were over.

When I finally got off the treadmill, my legs felt rubbery and I was sweating more than I ever remember sweating before. On top of that, I began to feel dizzy, and the room seemed to spin ever so slightly. My first thoughts were that I was feeling this way because I had overdid it without having the proper rest and not eating anything for breakfast, but when the thought that I may be having a heart attack quickly entered my mind, all I could do was drink some water and start thinking I may soon pass out. I just couldn't think of any other reason why I felt this way, and it really began to scare me. So much in fact that I even walked out into the lobby and told a young man there working behind the front desk what had just happened, and that I may pass out because of it. I then went to an area that had a few breakfast items sitting out and sat down there still sweating profusely and feeling dizzy. However, when I didn't begin to feel better, I became even more frightened that I had indeed injured my heart from the overexertion.

At this point, I noticed that some people were staring at me sitting there in my shorts and a t-shirt sweating like I was, but I didn't care one bit and soon made my way to the breakfast bar to make a bowl of cereal in hopes that eating something would help. After I sat back down, though, I could only eat a few bites of it, as my stomach was upset from being so scared. Finally, I just gave up and went back to the room to tell my wife what had happened. She told me I had probably just worked out too hard, and to drink something with sugar in it, which I did. Hearing her tell me I had simply just worked out too hard comforted me somewhat, but it didn't bring much relief from the fear I was feeling—a fear that would soon overwhelm me, and begin the worst period I ever experienced in my sobriety.

On our way home from Pittsburgh that afternoon, we stopped on the turnpike to eat lunch. I wasn't hungry because I was still feeling scared about what happened that morning, but when I told my wife this, she said I still needed to try and eat something anyway. After receiving our order, we all sat down in the crowded area to eat our food, and after only one bite from the cheeseburger I had ordered, I immediately felt like gagging. Nevertheless, I still managed to swallow it, and slowly take another smaller bite after that one. Unfortunately for myself and the other people around me, this bite turned out be a big mistake. I gagged so loud after taking it that everyone looked over at us. If it would have stopped there this may not have been too embarrassing, but I felt I really needed to finish this burger to hopefully start feeling better from working out so hard that morning, and after I finally managed to swallow that piece, I took yet another small bite. This time however, not only did I gag out loud again, but I kept on gagging with each one getting louder than the one before. By now my daughter and her friend, along with my son, were laughing hysterically at me, but my wife surely wasn't. She was telling me to go to the restroom instead of just sitting there gagging like that. At first I didn't go, but when I finally felt like I was actually going to throw up, I quickly made my way there to do just that.

I did get my appetite back the next day, but over a very short period of time after the "treadmill" incident, as the worry I had about having a heart attack started growing more into a fear that I had one, I also began to worry about something else, which was having colon cancer. I know this sounds crazy, and looking back now I certainly wouldn't argue, but at the time, since I did have a history of not being able to go to the bathroom properly and had to use laxatives at times to be able to do so, along with the fear I had about having a heart attack, made it easy for this worry to surface as well. Also, I couldn't just drink like I had in the past to push any fears or worries I had out of my mind. All I felt I could do was schedule a doctor's appointment to get checked out and hope this would bring me some peace of mind. I remember being there with my wife, who the whole time before this was trying her best to convince me there was nothing wrong with me and that it was all in my head, but still came along to support me. Once there, I couldn't wait to tell the doctor what happened on the treadmill, and how I thought I may have had a heart attack, but I was equally as eager to tell him about my bowel movement troubles. He was a very nice man of Asian nationality, and after telling him about what all I thought may be wrong, he checked my heart with his stethoscope, and did some other routine things including asking me questions. One of them was if after getting off the treadmill I felt like my heart was going to pop out of my chest, and when I said no, he actually chuckled before telling me in slightly broken English, "You're not going to die from anything then."

After that he asked me if I urinated a lot through the night, and when I answered yes and told him two or three times, he said that was a lot for a young man like myself and asked if I'd ever had my prostate checked. When I told him I hadn't, he told me he would check it now and asked if I wanted my wife to leave the room. I responded with a smile and answered by saying it didn't matter if she stayed since we have been through so many other things together, and a few minutes later, there I was lying on my side on the examining table, with my wife and I both laughing as the doctor went about the business of checking my prostate. Finally, when he was done, he told me everything seemed ok, and after I got myself together he handed me a kit to take along home to check my stool for blood. It came with instructions on how to use it and where to send it when I was done, and he told me his office would contact me with the results, but not to worry about anything because he felt I was a healthy young man. I left there feeling a little better, but even after getting his reassurance my heart was fine, in August I would go on our family vacation feeling worried and afraid that I'd had a heart attack.

We went to a beach in New Jersey we had gone to when the kids were younger and I wanted it to be fun for all of us, but it was hard for me to do so as I kept alternating from simple anxiety to outright fear worrying about my heart. I remember many times getting on my knees when I was alone and praying to God to make the fear go away, and although it would subside at times, it wouldn't go away entirely. I did as best I could under the circumstances to enjoy being with my family, though, and we did have fun by going to the beach and playing games on the boardwalk, but my wife could tell I was still feeling worried and afraid. A few days after we got back, just when I thought I couldn't feel much worse, a feeling of deep despair started and it didn't take long for a depression to set in. I then trudged through each day trying to feel as best I could, going to meetings and sharing with everyone about how I was feeling in hopes of hearing something back that would help me end this overwhelming fear that was causing me so much pain. This fear also affected my relationship with my wife. Although she tried to help me by constantly telling me I would be all right and getting me out of bed in the mornings when I was depressed, as I became more withdrawn and unresponsive to her, she eventually realized there was nothing else she could do for me and like so many other times when I was still drinking, she simply focused on our children and herself instead. Thankfully the depression would go away for good, and after a one-time visit to a psychologist, I felt enough reassurance to start believing I would be all right. I would come away from this experience with a much better understanding of why some people can become suicidal when in a depression. Not that I was suicidal myself, but because of how I so desperately wanted the fear and sadness to end.

Fortunately, through September as I kept praying and going to AA meetings, the fear and sadness did finally end, and I would realize that no matter how afraid I felt, I could at least stay sober. Through the rest of the year, even though I still occasionally worried this fear might return, I was fairly happy, but I would have other fears to deal with in 1998. Some would come from becoming a salesman at a higher-end electronics store where I would need to actually go to training to acquire the knowledge needed in order to sell the equipment, and some would come from an old familiar fear: jealousy—an adjective defined as being envious of someone else's achievements or advantages, or being resentful of someone regarded as a sexual rival. Although by this time I pretty much stopped having most of the jealousy described in that first definition that I had about people who were wealthy or who had a more prominent job than me, I did become very jealous of another man.

Around the time I had gone through my concerns about my health, my wife slowly became much more involved in my daughter's singing career, and when my daughter started practicing with a new band sometime later that year, my wife quickly became friends with all of the band members. Eventually she was with them so much that by the time I started my new job, she had became close to a few of them, but when I begin to feel she was getting too close to one member in particular, my jealousy kicked in and the resentment started. I would eventually see that my wife wasn't anything more than a friend to this person, but sadly at the time I really thought she was having an affair with him, and this almost caused us to separate. My wife learned much later in my sobriety that I did some things at this time that weren't very spiritual, like checking her e-mails to read the messages she would send to the band member asking him about when the band's play dates were and things of that nature. However, I felt a few of these e-mails were more personal than they needed to be. One of them in particular that she sent had to do with her going to his house to sew a pillow for him. Now this was actually a pillow that belonged to a couch we had given to him, but I didn't like the idea of my wife going to any man's house and sewing anything for him.

The second thing I did was a direct result from reading the e-mails she sent him, and probably the craziest thing I ever did in my sobriety. I remember a few days after reading them, I just happened to notice a key on her key chain that I didn't recognize from before. Now in my insecure and jealous state of mind, between the e-mails and finding this strange key, I became suspicious that this key may well belong to the band member's house. After finding the key, I took it off the key chain and left the house to go find out if the key fit. Soon I was standing on this man's front porch, knocking on his door and ringing the doorbell to see if anyone was home, not knowing what I would say if he answered, but wanting to make sure no was there before I tried the key. Finally, when I was sure no one was inside, I pulled the key from out of my pocket and stood there debating if I wanted to try it or not. After a minute or two of standing there with my heart racing, I decided to try it, and after I nervously put the key in place and pushed it forward it actually did fit the lock. A sudden feeling of dread came over me after this, but fortunately it was fleeting as only a split second after inserting the key I also tried to turn it, and of course it wouldn't turn. Although this gave me some feeling of relief, it would still take more than a key not turning in a lock to end the suspicions I had about my wife having an affair.

Thankfully, however, they would begin to subside after an AA meeting in which I talked to someone about them. The amazing part about why they began to subside, though, is that after listening to me go on about the things I did, and about how I afraid I was of losing my wife because of being so untrusting of her, all this person needed to say to me was, "Darryl, your wife's not going to leave you," and I immediately began to feel that she was probably right, and everything was going to be ok. This person was a woman that I had grown to trust and love, and she had said this with such heartfelt conviction that I simply believed her. Sadly, around a year after this she died, and I will never forget her. She was one of the most spiritual people I have ever met, and no matter how bad her financial or personal circumstances were, she never complained. She's also one of the reasons I began trying to believe everything's going to be all right even when it's not, as she was certainly proof that someone can be all right no matter what their circumstances. I still remember how spiritual she remained even after losing the bottom portion of one of her legs to diabetes, and eventually having to go to the hospital for heart troubles. The hospital, however, is the place where she would leave this world to go be with the God she often talked about in meetings and that she never once seemed to doubt existed. I always felt this wonderful presence around her because of the love that she showed to me and everyone else she knew, and I realize today that this was because somewhere along her journey of spiritual growth, she had already learned to love herself.

For me, however, it would take much more practice at trying to be a better person than I was before to even begin liking myself. I would begin doing that after that AA meeting by trying harder to overcome the jealousy with my wife and instead showing her more love and kindness, and also by attempting to overcome any new fears I felt through this time. Although they weren't nearly as bad as the ones I experienced in my second year sober, they nevertheless made me feel unhappy, and I would use my false sense of ego to help me get through them, like when I had to go to the sales training classes required by the high-end electronics store. I attended them a few months after I began working there and because the training was for six weeks, it scared me that I would have to be away for training every week, and only home on the weekends. I can still remember feeling lonely and afraid while being there, especially when I was in the motel room where I stayed by myself. Fortunately, there was an AA meeting in the next town that I could drive to in the evenings after training let out in order to help me get through how I was feeling. I would go directly there, and share with everyone how I felt like a frightened little boy who was away from home for the very first time. Just admitting this would help me feel a little better, as would hearing other people share about their own fears. But what really made me feel better was when someone sober longer than me would share and reassure everyone that although they too had fears on some days that they were much better at dealing with them now, and that they were happy in their lives today. Then when the meeting was over I would go get something to eat and take it back to the motel room, where I would remain for the night. This fear didn't stop me, however, from playing the wise-cracking funny guy while I was at training.

Although everyone there was much younger than me, they enjoyed my humor and thought I was funny. Even the instructors liked my jokes and the antics I exhibited during training, but there were some days when I could tell they also had enough. In many ways, acting like this reminded me of when I was back in high school as I used my humor to help me overlook the fears and insecurities I felt. As time went by and training ended, although I returned to the store with more confidence than I had before, I still felt worried about my abilities to sell there. I would compensate for feeling this way by occasionally bragging about all the sales I would soon be making and keeping up the "tough guy identity" that was still so important to me. I had never completely given it up when I stopped drinking (except for the times when I was so scared I couldn't pretend to be anything, let alone a tough guy), because I still needed it to feel good about myself. By this time, however, I will say that the false sense of ego I used to help me pretend to be the "tough guy" was much more diminished than when I was drinking. This was a direct result from going to AA meetings and trying to practice The Twelve Steps of Alcoholics Anonymous as best as I could each day.

Unfortunately, though, this wouldn't be the case for some of the other things I still needed to work on with myself, like the negativity I would often still show. This was the same negativity that I always displayed in my drinking days whenever other people were positive about some event or situation that I didn't personally agree with. This negativity was first brought to my attention by someone I worked with in my second year sober, and I remember them saying to me that I wasn't happy unless something was wrong. I also remember my wife mentioning this negativity quite often as well back then, and my son actually calling me Mr. Minus Sign. Now here it was over a year later and once again this negativity was being brought to my attention by people I worked with who told me I complained too much when business was slow and about the way the company ran things.

Today I can see how I was definitely a much more negative person than I would have liked to have been back then, but even after it was once again being brought to my attention, I still didn't think I was. I thought I was truly justified in how I felt about these things, and although I would at least admit that I did complain too much, it would take a somewhat dramatic event late the following year to make me realize it. The rest of 1998 moved along without any incidents that I can remember as I kept going to AA meetings, practicing the Twelve Steps, and finally got over the jealousy I felt about my wife. Also near the end of that year, a new manager would take over the store, and although in the beginning we had some personality clashes, after I finally realized it was more related to my behavior than anything he was doing, and that he was just asserting his authority, we took a genuine liking to each other. As a matter of fact, by the time my fourth year sober began in April of 1999, we were actually good friends, which was a good thing, as sometime later that year I would end up testing his patience during a morning sales meeting.

This meeting was held almost every Saturday morning about an hour before the store opened, and before this one even began, I was already in a sour mood. The other salesmen and I already knew what the meeting was going to be about; changes were being made to how we would be paid on our sales commissions. None of us were too happy about this, but I quickly took it to a whole other level after the store manager began telling us how this change would be a good thing and we would make more money. Although we would start being paid more on all the audio equipment we sold, we would be paid less on all the video equipment we sold. Since most of our sales were video, this would, in my mind, obviously decrease our sales commissions. I wasn't the only one who wasn't happy about this change, but I was the only one getting angry about it and voicing my opinion. Eventually, the store manager, who for most of the meeting had been trying to humor me about the whole situation, finally got angry and told me I was overreacting. This made me feel even angrier, and, of course, I was also now mad at him for not seeing the situation the way I did. Finally, when the meeting was over, although I still didn't feel like I was overreacting to the changes, I asked my close friend who worked there if he thought I was. What followed finally made me realize I was a negative person.

When my friend said that yes, I was overreacting, I shouted at him to get away from me before I knocked him on his ass. The store manager, who by now knew me much better, ran up to me and told me to go turn on the stereo equipment and to calm down while I did so. After some time had passed, he did something funny that I will never forget. He walked into the audio room where I was standing and staring straight ahead, thinking about what had just happened, and he stood there right beside me without saying a word. After about a minute or so, I realized he was actually imitating me by also staring straight ahead, but with a forlorn look on his face in an attempt to make me laugh. It worked almost immediately and after a few seconds, he turned to me and said I should probably go home for the rest of the day, but that if I wanted to come back later and talk to him about what was bothering me, I could. Considering how I behaved all through the meeting and the way I yelled and threatened my friend, any other manager would have surely fired me that day, but he didn't. He had known for some time that I was an alcoholic and I think this helped him to understand that despite my behaviors that morning, I really was trying to become a better person.

I needed this experience to make me realize I wasn't as happy in my life as I wanted to be, and I made even more progress after another event. This was a surprise party thrown for me by my wife in January, 2000 to celebrate my 40th birthday. Since it was held almost a whole month after my actual birthday, it certainly was quite a surprise! It was held at a private club my wife and I were once members of that served cheap food and alcohol, and I frequently went there in my drinking days. Now, however, we only went there for dances and parties with some friends who belonged.

My wife told me we were going there for a dance that night, and as I walked downstairs to an area of this place, truly believing there was a dance going on, I heard people yell, "Surprise!" and my mouth dropped open as I realized this was really a surprise party for me. It brought tears to my eyes as I began to look around the room and see how many people were there. I also remember wondering how many people would have shown up for a party for me when I was drinking. I truly believe that this night was needed to help me realize I was becoming a better person than I was before and I needed this night to start liking myself and feeling happier because of it.

These feelings would continue after that night and although there were still times when I bragged about some of my sales and occasionally acted like a tough guy, I would keep trying to be a better person than I was before. In April I would celebrate my fourth year sober and I recall that this was the year I first realized I had grown more spiritual. I had started going to a different AA meeting than before. The reason I had changed was because there always seemed to be some kind of drama going on either with one of the members or about something that happened there and because I had created enough of my own dramas in my drinking days, I decided I didn't need to be around someone else's at this point in my sobriety. One evening at this new meeting, out of nowhere, I began crying while sharing. After this meeting ended, a man with many years of sobriety approached me and asked me with what sounded more like a statement than a question, "You're an emotional guy, aren't you?" I answered back somewhat sheepishly with, "Yeah, I guess I'm still a little immature in my emotions," and that's when he said something I'll never forget, something that not only made me feel better about crying in the meeting, but to never be ashamed to cry at all. He looked me right in the eyes and said very softly, "You're just speaking the language of the heart, and it's okay to cry."

At first I wasn't sure just how sincere he really was in saying this until he added that he could hear the honesty in my voice as I was speaking with such emotion, and that he liked what I had shared. To this day I don't remember what it was I was sharing about when I started crying, but I do believe I know why it began at this particular time. By this time, I had acquired a lot of gratefulness for remaining sober through the fear I felt from the "treadmill" incident and the jealousies I had about my wife. And after, realizing I was becoming a better person than I was before I started liking myself and feeling happier in life. I think this combination of feelings made me cry that night while sharing at the meeting, and I would continue to do so at other meetings. Furthermore, I believe this day was needed for me to come to believe that God works through people, and that this experience was needed for me to realize I had grown more spiritual.

I would continue to go to that meeting for a little while longer, but in September, I would change to one that would end up being my Home group. It was called this if you considered it to be the main meeting you went to, which I did. I went there on my day off work, but I also occasionally went during work if for some reason I felt sad or afraid that day. From what I remember, though, I wouldn't feel that way too much for the rest of this year, as I remained fairly happy and content, but in January of 2001, those feelings would quickly come to an end after I decided I wanted to get out of retail sales and find a new job. The idea of doing this started only a few days into the new year after me and my good friend who worked there were talking about how much we really wanted to get out of retail sales that year. We realized some of the reason for feeling this way came from the fact that we had just worked all those long holiday hours and felt burnt out, but we both agreed we had been in the business long enough and needed a change. Also, I was growing tired of working almost every weekend and missing out on attending various family and social functions with my wife. Here I was sober for almost five years and happier than at any other time I could remember, but I still wasn't enjoying my life as much as I wanted too. Besides that, having just turned 41 in December, although I was in decent shape for my age, standing on my feet all day was starting to wear me out.

All of this only convinced me more that day that it was time to get out of sales, but I knew it wouldn't be easy. For one thing, I didn't have the skills needed for most other jobs, and for another, I didn't have a college degree. Although I admit this really worried me, I still tried to believe that with God's help, a job opportunity would eventually come along, and scheduled a two-week vacation starting the third week of January to get away for a while. This initially made me happy, but over the next week and half as I awaited my vacation, this happiness rapidly diminished as the worry I felt about finding a job grew worse, and for the first time in my sobriety, I even began to have doubts about God helping me. When this doubt caused me to feel afraid, I prayed even more for God to help me, and when it was time to leave for vacation, I left hoping that if I continued to pray and went to AA meetings I'd be all right.

I don't remember how I felt over that first week of vacation, but I know as the second week began, I was feeling quite sad. By Wednesday morning, I remember waking up and actually feeling depressed. So much, in fact, that I wound up standing in my kitchen looking out the back door at the other townhouses in my development, thinking how unimportant I felt in my life by living there and just being a salesman at an electronics store. Soon after this, I started wondering what the purpose to my life even was, and I started to cry. Only a few seconds later, I began to think that maybe there wasn't any purpose to life at all, and that maybe there wasn't even a God. As I stood there still looking out the door with the impact of that last thought slowly sinking in, a fear like I had never felt before came over me and I started crying even harder. I turned away from the door with tears streaming down my face and walked to the other side of the kitchen, and no sooner had I got there, a feeling that I can only describe as an emptiness inside took shape, and I dropped to my knees right where I was standing and cried out, "Are you there God? Are you really there?" I'm not sure if I actually expected an answer after this, but I did remain on my knees crying for awhile, hoping for some kind of sign. When that didn't happen, I got up and knew right away I needed to go to my AA Home Group meeting that afternoon in hopes of hearing something that would restore the belief in God I had only a few minutes before if I wanted the fear and emptiness to go away.

After going there, however, and sharing about what happened that morning, although many people shared afterwards why they believed there was a God or a Higher Power, some doubts still remained, and so did the fear and emptiness. Because of this I went to another meeting that evening, but once again after sharing what had happened and listening to the people share back why they believed there was some sort of God, the doubts didn't fully go away and I went to bed that night still feeling the same way. After doing the same thing again the next day, though, I actually left the last meeting feeling a lot better than I had before, and although I still felt afraid and empty inside, I went to bed that night with hope that my faith would return.

When I got up the next morning with that hope still there, I prayed to whatever God there may be for my faith to return, and when it was time to leave for my Home Group meeting later, I felt even more hopeful that it would. After I got there, I didn't share right away, but sat there listening to other people, hoping to hear anything that would make me believe in a God again. About halfway through the meeting, someone shared that they truly believed there was a reason for why everything happened in their life the way it did. I remember looking out of one of the six windows across the room from where I was sitting and thinking then there has to be a reason for what I was going through now.

As I continued looking out the window, before I even thought about what the reason for it could possibly be, a conviction that there truly was one came over me and the fear I had been feeling was replaced by one of comfort.

Immediately after that, the thought that there had to be some kind of God entered my mind, and then right after that, my belief that there was a God returned and the emptiness I had been feeling was gone. I knew at that point I just had to tell everyone about it, and sat there with much anticipation until I got my chance. Finally, when I was called on, I started out in the beginning by telling everyone what happened that Wednesday morning, and how I had gone to meetings every day hoping to hear something that would make my belief in God return. After I told them how during this meeting my faith returned, I began crying as a feeling of gratefulness overwhelmed me and for a few moments all I could do was sit there in silence as tears ran down my face.

When I was finally able to continue, I went on to explain to everyone that I thought it was by going to those meetings and hearing so many people share how their lives had become so much better since they quit drinking and how they believed it could've only come about because of a God or a Higher Power that I was eventually able to have hope that my faith would return. I then went on to say that I thought it had to be that hope that made it possible for my belief in God to return as quickly as it did, and ended with how grateful I was for it. I don't remember what anyone shared after I was finished, but when the meeting was over, some people came up to give me hugs. I feel this day was needed for me to begin to believe there truly is a reason for why everything happens in life, and I needed to realize I could use hope to help fight any doubts and fears I may have along the way.

I would need to try and believe that first statement even more the very next day, when I discovered I still felt unimportant in my life by living where I did and being a salesman. Oddly enough, the reason for feeling this way had something to do with a famous actress—Julia Roberts. I watched her win a Golden Globe the Sunday before that traumatic morning when I lost my faith, and after that I simply became infatuated with her. I tried to learn as much as I could about her, rented some of her movies to watch that week even though I had already seen some of them before, and tuned into the entertainment shows every evening in hopes of seeing her again. However, after reading somewhere that she was a decent and down-to-earth human being who gained more happiness in life from being a good person than she did from being a famous movie star, this infatuation turned into a genuine fondness and admiration for her.

Although I could now see it was these feelings that were behind the unimportance I felt in my life, I still didn't understand why, and simply told myself there had to be a reason for it and hoped it would soon pass. It wouldn't though, and after I returned to the electronics store the following week, it actually became more intense. After that day, the deep sadness returned, and by the end of the week I knew I would have to get over this whole Julia Roberts thing if I wanted to be happy again. I did this by praying to God to help me and going to AA meetings, which helped me to feel better on some days, but as February went by, the feeling of unimportance remained and the sadness would always return. I did find something else that temporarily made me feel better, which was playing a game called Cranium with my wife and friends that I read Julia Roberts liked to play. When I first learned she liked this game, I immediately went out and purchased it and found out it was a lot fun. I wasn't sure why it made me feel better playing it, but as crazy as it may sound to some people, it helped me to feel better about myself and get through some of my sadness. Finally, near the end of February after sharing something at a meeting that I know definitely sounded crazy even to people in AA, some events would take place that would help give me a better understanding of why I was feeling this unimportance and sadness in my life and enable me to start feeling happier.

I went to a meeting that day to share about what I was going through, as usual, but this time I decided to also share a part I had been leaving out. I told everyone about how my feelings for Julia Roberts were somehow behind the unimportance I felt, and as if that didn't already sound crazy

enough, I also told them that because of all of this I was now
thinking about becoming an actor. I had actually started to
think about it a few days before, but I had been too
embarrassed to share about it. Now that I did however, I
didn't feel the least bit embarrassed, and actually felt a little
better. I don't recall what anyone may have shared after
hearing this, but it may not have sounded as crazy as I
thought.

When the meeting was over, a man I had talked to a
few times in the past came up to me to offer some help. This
was unusual for him to do so, but because of what I had
shared he thought he would suggest me going to a small
local theater in our area to see about a part in a play.
Although I had already thought about this myself, I didn't
want to hurt his feelings and thanked him for his help. We
talked a little more about it, said our goodbyes, and I left to
go home. On my way home, the idea of becoming an actor
began to quickly fade away. I had known deep inside since I
first thought about going to this place that I would be too
afraid to go and try out, but because the idea of being an
actor made me feel better about myself, I fooled myself into
believing I would. I had grown more spiritual by trying to be
a better person than I was before, but I hadn't grown a whole
lot in my self-confidence and as a result, what I was
experiencing was a feeling of inferiority to Julia Roberts. I
had simply been seeing her as a famous movie star who was
very confident in herself and talked about how much she
loved her job as an actress, while thinking of myself as some
salesman no one ever heard of who hated his job. This all
came to me that day, and although the feeling of unimportance remained, I started feeling happier and was able to
think about Julia Roberts without feeling as inferior as
before. It would be after reading something about her a few
weeks later, though, that I would finally begin to feel better
about just being a salesman. I came across something in a
magazine that basically reiterated what I had learned about
her that week after the Golden Globe Awards, that she was a
decent human being who gets more happiness in life from

being a good person than she does from being a famous movie star.

This was a major revelation for me, because it opened up my eyes to something that I had been overlooking the whole time I was going through this—that I was also a decent person who gained his happiness from trying to be a better person, and right after this revelation, I started feeling a little better about living in a small townhouse and just being some salesman. Without ever meeting her, Julia Roberts simply being the person she was had in some strange way helped me feel good about myself, and the feeling of unimportance would soon go away. By now it was mid-March and I was feeling much happier with that all behind me, but I did experience some sadness when I learned the manager who understood me would be leaving to take a different position in the company.

The night before he left, everyone from the store got together after work at a nearby bar and restaurant to say their goodbyes, and as the night went on, some people got drunk and with full emotion told him they would miss him, but I think I was the only one who had tears in his eyes after telling him this. It took me a few days to cheer up after he was gone, and a little while to adjust to the new manager, but by the end of the month I now felt good enough about myself to be able to watch Julia Roberts win an Oscar for best actress without feeling inferior to her.

As April went by, although my false sense of ego would occasionally flare up and I'd act like a tough guy, I also continued trying to be a better person than I was before, and was fairly happy as things went well for me both at work and at home with my wife and son. At the end of April, however, when I went to my Home Group AA meeting to speak for my fifth year anniversary sober, I experienced a lot of unhappiness when I first got there. I had been going there for around eight months already and because I thought my sharing made an impact on people at the meetings, there would be a lot of people there, but there wasn't. I was off from work that day and got to the meeting around fifteen minutes before it started; I was very nervous, and went to the bathroom before going upstairs to the room where the meeting was always held.

As I walked into the room, I saw there were only about six or seven people there. This hurt my feelings, especially when a couple of people that I had thought would be there weren't. I tried not to let it show, though, and took my seat in front of the room where I would be sharing, but I have to say at this point I was actually thinking about leaving. But because I knew it was the thing to do, I stayed, and as the remaining minutes ticked away, I kept thinking there had to be a reason for me to be there. I was still upset even after a few more people showed up, and didn't even listen as the Twelve Steps and other AA literature were read aloud. Finally, when it was time for me to begin speaking, I sat there and looked around the room at the sparse crowd, and you know what I did? I told everyone exactly how I had been feeling since I first walked into the room, and began to cry as I went on to say that I had almost left because of it. I told them that one of the reasons I stayed was because I believed there was a reason for why things happen the way they do in our lives, and thought maybe I needed to experience this. I then added that at that very moment while I was talking to them, I was actually beginning to feel better, and that this was something else that I believed in—to talk about your true feelings and not hold them in. I told them another reason I stayed was because I was trying to be a better person than I was before. It came to me that what was helping me sit there and tell them all of this was the spiritual growth I had acquired from trying to do so. I told them I believed this was why I was meant to have this experience.

What amazed me was that in the beginning, everyone had sat there with a look of disbelief on their faces, but as I went on, their expressions slowly changed and became looks of genuine interest. At this point, I made some small joke about the whole thing, and after everyone laughed, I went on to tell my story. Finally, as the hour was coming to an end, I finished up by telling them how trying to be a better person than I was before had also helped me to like myself, and that I had become much happier in my life because of it. After I was finished speaking, almost all of them commented on the things I had just shared with them. And when some of them mentioned how much they liked my honesty and the way I had been so open. Tears came to my eyes and I was glad I stayed. Before the meeting officially ended, the coins, called "chips" in AA, that mark how long someone has been sober were handed out. When it was my turn, I proudly accepted one for being sober for five years.

I would soon feel a different kind of pride when in the beginning of May, a "hot shot" salesman was hired at the electronics store. He was a good-looking, taller, younger man in his late twenties with dark hair, who in only a short time began outselling everyone there, including me. At first, because I was trying to be more spiritual, I told myself it didn't matter and tried not to let it bother me. But when he kept outselling me and everyone else, as much as I tried not to let it affect me, it did, and sometime in June, I finally let it show. After hearing about some big sale he just made, my pride got the best of me, and as my "false sense of ego" flared up, I said in front of him and some of the other salesman, "I'm done being outsold, and it's going to end." Fortunately for me, when it didn't end and he continued to outsell me, I was able to realize something important about myself that would help me to soon get out of retail sales. What I realized was that I just didn't have the drive to be a top salesman anymore because deep down I no longer cared as much about being one. I also realized that because of this, it was definitely time for me to get out of sales, and this time I would at least make an effort to find a different job.

The first thing I thought about was to try and become a nurse, but when that turned out to be financially impossible, I thought about maybe working in a retirement home for the sick and elderly. My wife, however, quickly interjected at that point and soon made me understand that I wasn't cut out for that level of caring. Then, as June was coming to a close, the good friend I worked with told me about a position he had been thinking about taking as a customer service rep at a wireless cell phone company. The reason he didn't say anything until now was because it didn't pay nearly as well as our sales job, and the company wasn't even sure if they were going to hire another person or not. After he saw how frustrated I was about not finding a job, however, he thought he would at least mention it to me. I immediately called the store manager there to see about the job, and he told me that he still didn't know for sure if the company was going to hire anyone else or not, but that I could still come in for an interview. I had my interview that week, and he told me that hopefully the company was going to let him know within the next couple of weeks if they were definitely going to hire another person, and if they were, I would get the job. I left excited about the prospect of working there, and tried to have hope that everything would work out the way I wanted it to, but because I did have some worries about the outcome, it soon started a tug of war with my emotions.

On most days, I was able to push the doubts out of my mind and feel all right, but there were some days when doubts about getting the job led to doubts about God helping me in my life and I'd feel afraid and sad. I would pray to God anyway on those days to help me get the job, and go to AA meetings to help me feel better. I would also find something else that would help me feel better, and once again I don't believe this was a coincidence.

Sometime in July, my wife and I drove to a bordering state to go shopping at a mall there. I stayed with her for awhile, but since I'm not the shopping type, I left her to go to a bookstore for something to do. The reason I really wanted to go, though, was because I was feeling some doubts and fears that day about getting the job and wanted to find something spiritual to read to hopefully make me feel better. After finding a section dedicated to spirituality, I began reading the titles of various books, and eventually came across one by an author who claimed to have had a conversation with God. I picked it up and after only reading a few pages, I knew I had to buy it. It spoke of many different things and answered many questions about life, but what struck me as most interesting was its constant referring to God as being a creator that gave us the ability to create our lives the way we wanted to through our thoughts.

Although I wasn't sure that the author had really talked to God, almost everything I read seemed to make sense to me and made me feel better that day. Because of this, I would continue to read this book whenever I had any doubts and fears about God helping me get the job at the cell phone company, trying as hard as I could to believe that I would get it. This must have helped because around the third week of July, I finally got a phone call from the manager at the cell phone store and he told me that I basically had the job, but that I still needed to talk to someone in the human resources department and answer a few questions before an official offer would be made. I was so excited as I thanked him for his part in all of this and after we said goodbye, I called the person he told me to, who just wanted to make sure I was all right with the requirements of the job and what it paid. Although it was indeed a lot less than what I had been making at the electronics store, I knew it was enough to pay my bills, and when they asked me if I wanted to come on board, I said yes. We then set a starting date, and I thanked them for the job.

After I hung up, I immediately called my wife to tell her the good news. Once again, I have to say that like so many other things in my life, I believe getting this job at the cell phone company wasn't a mere coincidence, as it would afford me the experiences needed to continue to grow spiritually and begin to love myself. I started working there the first week in September, and although there would be none of these experiences right away, a few helped me to become a more patient person than I was before, like trying to learn the computer system used to assist people with their wireless accounts, and trying to be nice towards angry customers who came into the store and were nasty about problems they had. I would eventually get the hang of the computer system, but the angry customers would continue to be a weekly challenge and a chance for me to not only practice patience, but also understanding. The same thing would go for the three young ladies that worked there, but we got along fine and I enjoyed working with them.

Near the end of the year, some of that enjoyment would temporarily vanish after I learned that everyone would have to work longer hours over the Christmas holidays, both at the store and a nearby mall where a stand would be set up for us to sell our phones. No one wanted to work these longer hours, especially at some stand in the mall, and I immediately began experiencing some of my old negativity. However, over the next couple of weeks before we were scheduled to begin working the longer hours, I at least tried to develop a more positive outlook about the whole thing, and when the longer hours started sometime in December, I did my best to try to be happy. This didn't last long, though, as there were no customers at the store during the later hours, and the mall was usually dead, so we didn't sell many phones. This whole experience quickly made me feel down, and I began reading another book from the author who claimed to have talked to God in an effort to make me feel better while having to be at the mall.

It was actually the second book of a trilogy, and once again it talked of how God was a creator and that we had the ability to create our lives the way we wanted to, but this one also went on to explain some of the deeper mysteries of life. I still wasn't sure if any of the things I read were true, but once again I found that reading about these things would help make me feel better. Finally, as the holidays passed and 2002 began, I felt happy as things went fairly well in my life. This would change around the beginning of April after I tried to help one of the young girls at work with some troubles she and her husband were having. She had grown close to me after I started working there, and had already confided in me about having some of these troubles back when we were working at the mall. She had also told me she was pregnant back then, and was now only a few months away from having her baby. She had been coming to work upset and crying for days, and this time when I talked to her about her current circumstances, I responded much more from the emotions I felt towards her because she was so upset. By doing this, I wasn't as kind as I should have been about her husband's role in the whole situation, and the next day she said she didn't appreciate me saying some of the things I did about him. I felt bad and apologized for whatever I said that offended her, but it didn't help, and she even stopped talking to me. After a couple of weeks of this, although I was trying to be a better person than I was before, some of the old Darryl in me surfaced from the hurt and resentment I was feeling, and there were times when I would say some things to her that weren't very nice.

This obviously didn't help the situation, and I felt so bad about the things I said I ended up sharing about it at an AA meeting. Later that month, I would also share at another speaker's meeting at my Home Group for my sixth year anniversary, and this time the room would actually be filled with people. This made me feel a whole lot better than the year before when so few people had shown up and I remember someone who had attended my last anniversary saying what a difference a year made. I laughed and agreed with them and this would be a very happy day for me. Over the next few weeks, I wouldn't feel so happy, though, as the way I had behaved towards the young girl was still making me feel bad and I knew I needed to be kind to her no matter how I felt. I remember sitting down one day and writing this young lady a four-page letter telling her how much I cared about her, and explained as best as I could how ridiculous this all was considering our past relationship. I then went on to tell her how I was also feeling hurt from the way she was treating me, and ended it by once again telling her how sorry I was over the whole thing. Later that day I put the letter on her desk where I was sure she would read it, and over the next few weeks I left her alone as much as I could, and showed her the kindness I should have from the very beginning.

Finally, just as she started to at least act more civil towards me, June had arrived and before anything was resolved between us, she would leave to go have her baby and be a stay-at-home mother. It hurt that she left without any true reconciliation, but not long after she had a little boy, I least was able to say hello to her and see the baby whenever she came into the store to show him to the girls. I would deliberately walk over to her each time to do this, and after awhile I was able to initiate short conversations with her. After doing this for several weeks and talking to her a little more each time, she actually came to me first one day and asked me how I was doing. After we exchanged pleasantries, she looked at me and blurted out that she was sorry for acting the way she did towards me and that she wasn't even sure why she had done it. I told her not to worry about it and that I was the one who should be sorry for the way I behaved. Then as we stood there looking at each other we both started grinning and when I leaned in and hugged her, she didn't hesitate to hug me back.

Although we had a rough patch there for awhile and I wasn't the most spiritual person through some of it. I believe this day was needed to see how important it was to practice things like love, kindness, and understanding in our lives. It also made me believe even more that there's a reason for everything that happens in our lives and for the people we meet. Like, for example, when I got to know the girl who started working there right after that young girl left. I remember we hit it off right away, and only a few days after she started working there, she confided in me that she was gay. I think it helped that right before she told me this, we were having a conversation about homosexuality in which I had expressed how it didn't bother me if someone was gay and that I believed people were born that way, and over time we would have many more conversations about homosexuality that would help deepen my understanding of it. We would also have conversations about the mysteries of life and our beliefs about God, and we became very good friends.

I was already friends with the person who took over as manager in July. We had met each other at some of the mandatory training classes given by the company and had fun together. She was a tall, stout woman with black hair and I think because she liked the little boy tendencies I sometimes showed, it helped us get along after she became my boss. As that year went on, I was happy both at work and at home, and not having to work at the mall over the holidays made Christmas that much better. The following year, in January 2003, there was another young lady, just twenty-one years old, hired at the store; she was so nice and pleasant to be around that I would occasionally tell her that if I was her father, I'd be proud to have a daughter like her. I would also continue having deep conversations with my lesbian friend, and continue my friendship with the only original girl still there since I started, and as the year moved on, it was beginning to be my best year yet sober. Everything was going good at work, my wife and I were getting along better than we ever had before, and although I would feel a sadness on some days, I was now pretty happy in my life. In fact, by April, despite occasional negativity and humorous sarcasm, because of my spiritual growth, I now felt I was a good person and rarely used my false sense of ego to feel better about myself.

I would talk about some of this and the experiences I had through my sobriety at my Home Group at the end of April where I shared for my seventh year anniversary. This would mark the first time that my wife was ever at one of my speaker meetings, but I didn't hold anything back as I was sharing and cried several times while telling my story. When I was finished, I told everyone there that although I still did things I didn't like myself for, I knew I was a good person, and as tears came to my eyes, I told them that I loved myself. I went on to explain how by trying to be a better person than I was before, I had grown spiritually, and this enabled me to love myself. I then added how grateful I was for The Twelve Steps of Alcoholics Anonymous because without them, none of this could have been possible. After this, some people shared how much they liked hearing me speak and that they got a lot out of what I said, and a couple of them told me how much it touched them when I cried throughout my story. I had actually seen a few people cry as I was speaking, too, and of course, my wife was one of them.

For the next month or so, I would continue to be very happy, but in June, things started changing at the cell phone store. They wanted us to go out and promote new business plus call customers to try and get them to add another cell phone to their account. I started having days when I didn't like working there anymore. Since April, all of us had already been taking turns working at a well-known retail electronics store that carried our phones in order to try and drum up new customers and although we weren't very happy about it, we had adjusted. However, by now having to do these other things on top of that, it made everyone angry and more unhappy; especially me. I felt I had come to the cell phone store to be a customer service rep, not a salesman, and although I did these things and tried to make the best out of it, I soon became resentful. It wasn't long after this that I began to experience a familiar feeling of sadness in my life, and when some of my old feelings of unimportance also began to surface, I no longer felt content there. It was these feelings that caused me to begin thinking about leaving there and pursing a dream that I had for some time now, which was to be a drug and alcohol counselor.

Although it scared me to think about leaving my job, as the feelings of sadness and unimportance grew and I actually hated being there, it drove me to at least start trying to find out what I would need to do to make my dream happen. I was amazed at how afraid I was to even begin doing this, and after I found out where I needed to go if I actually decided to pursue a career as a drug and alcohol counselor, I once again started to experience some doubts about God helping me in my life. Thankfully, because I had become better at handling my doubts and fears, I was able to tell myself I'd be all right, and I was able to hold onto my faith by praying and going to AA meetings. I also began reading the third book from the author who claimed to talk to God, and I occasionally talked to my lesbian friend about what I was going through. It would actually be after talking to her at work one day that I would see a connection to when I had also felt this sadness and unimportance at the electronics store. I had already told her about the time I lost my faith and about the fear and emptiness I felt back then, but I had never mentioned the unimportance I felt at that time and the whole Julia Roberts thing.

I picked a time when we could talk without being interrupted and then went ahead and told her the whole story, and after I was done, I asked her what she thought of Julia Roberts. She said she thought she was a good actress, and like me, felt she was a good person. Then I asked her how she would feel if Julia Roberts came into the store. She told me that she would feel intimidated, but also very excited to meet her, and then she asked me the same question. I already knew how I would feel—I had already been thinking about this earlier and answered that I would be embarrassed to have Julia Roberts come in and see me working there. I could see by her reaction to my answer that it puzzled her to hear this, and as we sat there looking at each other, I smiled because I knew she would ask me why. When she did, I told her that I really wasn't sure, but that I knew it somehow still had to do with the sadness and unimportance I felt. My friend really didn't know what to say, and we once again sat there looking at each other. This time she smiled at me and when she shrugged her shoulders to indicate she didn't have an answer for me, I shrugged mine too and we both got back to work.

I felt better after talking to her, but as I continued to think about why I would be embarrassed if Julia Roberts came into the store, I couldn't understand why at this point in my life I would feel this way. I had overcome most of the insecurities that made me feel inferior to other people and I truly felt I was good person now. Then as I thought back to when I had felt this unimportance in my life before through the "whole Julia Roberts thing," I began to see that just like now, it hadn't started until after I stopped liking where I worked and that I had felt very sad at that time too.

I would do my best to try and overcome the way I was feeling. It wouldn't be easy when we learned that there were going to be some major changes at the cell phone store. Although the company still wanted us to provide good customer service, they now felt the main priority should be for us to sell more mobile phones, and if this didn't happen, some people would no longer be needed. This news bothered me so much that I called the district manager to ask if people were really going to be let go if they didn't sell more phones. He told me that the company simply needed to make more money to survive, and that the only way to achieve this was by selling a lot more phones. He also told me very bluntly that if this didn't happen, "deadwood would have to go," and although this wasn't necessarily directed towards me, it hurt to hear it said like that.

The company had always been very family-oriented and seemed to go out of their way to make all their employees feel important, and now I was hearing how "deadwood would go" from someone that I had always liked and believed was a fair and decent person. In this conversation, he also told me that because of my sales experience, he expected me to be one of their top salesmen. Although I didn't say anything, I knew that this was going to be a problem, as I liked being a customer service rep a lot more than I did selling and had become quite satisfied helping customers. I remember thinking it was time to find another job. A few days later, this was confirmed when our store manager, who also wasn't happy with the changes, gathered us all together to tell us that our pay structures were going to change to mostly commission and that a meeting was scheduled for the first week in August to explain how it would work. After hearing this and still feeling quite resentful from the conversation I'd had with the district manager only a few days before, I remember walking out of the store and actually crying over the whole thing.

I immediately called my wife to tell her and after filling her in on everything in between the small sobs from my crying, I explained how I didn't want to be a salesman again because I knew I wouldn't be happy. The next thing I said came out of desperation: maybe I could ask some friends of ours who were wealthy if they would help me with some of the finances needed to go to college so I could get a degree as a Drug and Alcohol Counselor. She said I shouldn't ask them, and although it wasn't what I wanted to hear, I knew in my heart that as nice as these people were, she was right. Then, as it began to dawn on me that all of this was probably starting to worry her, I told her I agreed with her about this, and not to worry, that things would work out the way they're supposed to. She agreed. When we said goodbye, I stopped crying and went back into the store, I didn't talk to anyone as I tried to figure out why I had gotten so upset. I knew some of it was because of the emotions I had been feeling up to this time and some of it because I was tired of working at places that seemed to stop caring about the people that worked there.

As the day went on, I began to remember a few things that helped me understand why I had felt the way I did. First, I realized that as far back as 2001 I had wanted to do something different with my life, like helping others, and although working as a customer service rep at the cell phone company over the last two years had contented me, I still hadn't felt completely satisfied. I also realized that this had something to do with the fact that I had become a different person than I was before, and between realizing these things and the changes that were going to take place there very soon, it persuaded me to now face my fears and pursue my dream of becoming a drug and alcohol counselor. I remember getting very excited after scheduling an interview to talk to someone at a nearby community college to learn exactly what I would need to do to get a degree, and I couldn't wait to go there.

Back at the cell phone store, everyone was down because of all the changes that had taken place and because more changes were coming with how they would be paid, but I remained upbeat as I kept thinking that I would actually fulfill my dream of becoming a drug and alcohol counselor. Finally, sometime in August, I had the interview at the college where I was told what classes I would need to take in order to get an Associates Degree in Human Services, and how to apply for the loans and grants needed to pay for each semester. It only took a few weeks for me to get approved, and I figured out that along with my savings, I would have enough money from the loans and grants to be able to go to college. I knew this was going to severely strain our finances and I would have to work a part-time job, but I was I told at the interview that if I started in January of the following year and didn't miss any classes, it would be possible to obtain my Associates Degree in less than eighteen months. After getting the approvals and figuring my finances out, I decided I needed to quit the cell phone store because of the resentment I felt over the changes, and lined up another job as, believe it or not, a salesman.

The reason I decided to take this job, though, was because it was already September and I knew I would only have to work there for three months until my classes started. It also helped that I would be able to put some money away, because it paid a lot more than the cell phone job did. I must admit I was feeling some fear about taking this job, though, as it involved traveling long distances and trying to sell to businesses, but I was willing to face these fears, and started training the third week of September. This decision I soon regretted when less than two weeks after I started training, I found out that most of the people who worked there hated it, and that the owner was much more of a Mr. Hyde than a Dr. Jekyll. This prompted me to begin thinking about quitting there immediately, but since I would need money until I went to college, I didn't know what to do. However, after kicking around the idea of at least staying there one more week so I could collect a much higher training pay than what I would receive if I didn't complete the mandatory two-week training period, I decided that the right thing to do was to quit that day. I knew in my heart that I couldn't go to an AA meeting and face the people there if I did something devious like that, and I remember leaving there that day feeling good about myself for doing the right thing.

Fortunately I had some stocks that had been given to me free the year before from the company I had my life insurance through at this time and I was able to sell them for just enough money to hold me over until college started in January. Of course I knew I would still have to find a part-time job by then, but because of this I felt it wasn't a coincidence, and over the next few weeks it helped me to worry less about being unemployed. In October, this would change after another meeting with the college about the classes I was taking and the finances I had secured. After going over everything, the lady helping me told that a Bachelor's Degree would be needed to become a Drug and Alcohol Counselor; not an Associate's. I couldn't understand how information as important as this had eluded me at the previous meeting at the college, and as I sat there and listened to this nice lady tell me how an Associate's Degree in Human Services would only get me an entry level job in the drug and alcohol field, I just couldn't believe it. She then told me that I would have to go to a different college, as they didn't offer the classes there that I needed to be a drug and alcohol counselor, but at this point I knew it would cost more money than what I had and I just wanted to leave. When she was finished, I still managed to smile somehow and thank her, and quickly left to go to my car, feeling numb.

It was now pouring down rain and I was soaked by the time I got there, and as if this and the bad news wasn't already enough that day, after I started my car, a light on my dashboard came on indicating a light was out. It was a chore to replace the bulb and took several minutes of standing behind the car with the trunk open to do it, but because it was a brake light, I knew I should probably do so before I left and got out one of the spare bulbs I had just for this occasion. As I was in the process of doing so, I started thinking about what I had just learned inside and as a feeling of sadness hit me, I felt like crying. I held back, though, and when I was done replacing the bulb, I slammed the trunk shut, got back into the car, soaked even more now, and found my way out of the college parking lot to drive home. After I drove for awhile, still thinking about what I learned at the college, as it was slowly sinking in that my dream of being a drug and alcohol counselor was over, a feeling of despair came over me and the tears finally came. Although I began to realize this happened because of me not asking enough questions and misinformation when I initially applied at the college, I still wondered why it had to turn out this way. Then while still crying I asked out loud for God to give me an answer and when it didn't come, I'd once again find myself full of doubts and fears. Eventually this led me to search for proof in some kind of God, and like many other times in my life, a "coincidence" that I believe wasn't would occur and become the answer I asked for.

9

Why I began to believe in a Creator

"Is there a God?" and "Why are we here?" Are questions I've heard answers to many times throughout my life. Most of the time the answers came from people of faith who said there is a God, and that we're here to do His will. However there were other times when these answers came from people without faith who said there is no God, and life is what you make out of it. Although I was never religious, I guess I always believed there was some kind of God that helps us in our lives, and never worried about anyone's answers until I was forty-one years old. That's when with everything going good in my life, and being happier than at any other time I can remember, I started doubting that belief and soon found myself full of fear and feeling empty inside. With help this soon seemed to pass, but as the next few years went by and doubts in my belief still sometimes surfaced and made me feel afraid, it caused me to seek out reassurance there was a God, and for a purpose to our lives. And so far, at forty-four years old, although I'm still not entirely sure why we're here, I now have reason to believe there is something, a creator perhaps, that will explain to me what life is about after I die, and I pray to it in the shower.

I really don't remember exactly when I began praying in the shower, but I know it had to be sometime in 1999 after moving to the small townhouse that my wife and I still live in. It was a brand new home at that time and there was a big contrast between this place and the other one we had lived in for almost nine years. Besides the fact that we were buying the new place and had rented the other one, the new place was smaller with carpeted rooms, central air, and sat between two other townhouses with matching tan siding. The old place, although not really that much larger, had a few more rooms with wooden floors that were cold in the winter, needed window air conditioners in the summer, and was a brick Tudor that sat by itself. Also, even though the other place was nice and my wife decorated it to make it look even nicer, because it was an older home, it needed a lot of work, where the new place only needed my wife's loving touches.

There were, however, two other important differences worth mentioning. The new place wasn't filled with so many bad memories like the other one where my family and I had lived over the last six years of my drinking, and it had a brand new bathroom with a brand new shower. It actually had a half bath on the first floor as well, but the full bathroom upstairs was the one with the tub and shower where I soon began praying. When I was in this new shower with the warm water running down over me, I simply felt more at peace than I ever had in the other one. At first I thought it was because I didn't think about the bad memories like I had sometimes done while in the shower at the old house, but I found that even months later, I would still feel at peace while in this shower, and I continued getting down on my knees and talking to God there. I especially did a lot of this after that day I got the news at the college. I had tried to believe there was a reason for what happened and went to AA meetings and read more books about God to try and bring me some comfort, but none of it helped with the doubt and fear I was feeling.

It was because of this that I decided to search the Internet for some kind of proof in a God and to discover if there was a purpose for our lives. I began by typing something in the search bar like, "god" and "the universe" or "is there a God," and although a lot of what I found had to do with religion, there was also a lot of information on what science had to say about there being a God. I have to admit that some of what I found gave reasons as to why there wasn't a God and at times made me feel even more afraid, but two things that I learned about slowly made me feel there had to be something that created life and the universe for a reason. One was "The Big Bang Theory," which explained how the universe began, and the other one was something called Quantum Physics, which explained how everything comes into our existence. What was amazing to me was how all of this fit in with what I had already read in the books where the author had claimed to talk to God. Although I didn't grasp the full meaning of what I had read at this time, it nevertheless helped take away some of the doubts and fears I had, and filled me with newfound hope that there was a creator and that maybe I actually had the ability to overcome the fears I felt.

There was something else that helped make me feel better not long after reading about these things, and it went along way in helping me believe even more that there aren't any coincidences in life. My daughter, who had heard what happened at the college, called to tell me that she told her singing manager, and he told her about a detention home for troubled teenagers that might hire me as a counselor. He had apparently known about the place for some time and would often have the young men from the home come over to his music studio and learn about music and writing songs. I called him the next day to ask him some questions about the place, and after he answered what he could, he told me to come over to his studio the following week and meet the teenagers there. I jumped at the chance to do this and looked forward to going, but I really didn't know what to expect and I remember being very nervous about going there.

When the day finally came, my daughter's manager introduced me as a visitor to the teenagers and the counselors that had brought them, and I sat down to watch these young men as they learned more about music and finished up songs they had written. After awhile, some of them would come up to me to show me a song they wrote or just to say hello, and it immediately made me feel good. I considered joking around with them, but because I was feeling very nervous, I just sat there quietly instead. I did, however, begin to think how nice it would be to work with these teenagers, and even daydreamed about being some Super Counselor. Finally, when I had to go, I said goodbye to all the young men and briefly spoke to the counselor in charge, who gave me the information I needed to schedule an interview with the program director who ran the detention facility. This place was actually one of seven detention homes owned by one person where teenagers were sent to serve time for crimes they committed.

The next day, I called the place to set up an interview with the program director that would take place the following week. I remember actually driving there a few days beforehand to see exactly where it was, and was surprised to see that this detention home was an old farmhouse without bars; it was actually quite nice. Finally, the day came for my interview, and after I got there, I had to ring a buzzer for someone to come to the door. As I sat down on the couch to wait for the program director in what probably once had been a small living room, I looked out through what was an equally small dining area that had a long table on either side of it with many chairs, into what was obviously a kitchen. Sitting there waiting, I was again feeling very nervous, like when I first met the teenagers at the studio, but this would soon subside after I met the program director. As it turned out, I had helped him with a cell phone problem while I was still working at the cell phone store, and he remembered that not only was I helpful and kind to him, but how much it showed that I didn't care what color he was. He was a very big black man in his fifties, and very aware of the prejudice that unfortunately still plagued the area we lived in. As a matter of fact, this led to a lengthy conversation about racism in general, and it was quite interesting listening to his views on the subject.

Finally, we got around to what my qualifications were, and I knew that honesty was the best way to explain why I felt I would be a good counselor. I told him that while on paper I may not have many qualifications, I was an alcoholic and because over the last seven and half years I had worked The Twelve Steps to help myself and other Alcoholics, I had learned a lot about what people needed to do to become emotionally well. This is when he told me he actually ran a morning AA meeting on Saturdays where people who were caught for drunk driving had to attend as part of their sentences, and although he wasn't an alcoholic, he knew the AA program very well. Because of this, I immediately felt comfortable with opening up to him more about some of the things I now believed in, so I proceeded to tell him how I felt that a lot of what was written in the Twelve Steps could be used to help anyone, whether teenagers or adults. I then added that I believed that, by telling someone the troubles you've faced in your life and how you overcame them, it helped gain the trust needed for someone to open up and talk to you about their own troubles. I also told him that when this happened, even if someone wasn't sure why they had some of the problems they did, they at least had to admit that they weren't doing something right in life or they wouldn't be in the trouble they were in. I finished by saying how I believe when you help someone understand that it is really their fears, insecurities, and negative emotions that cause most of their problems and explain how talking about your emotions helps you to better understand them, that person can also begin to understand themselves and be all right in life.

He fully agreed, and when we were finally through with the interview, he told me he had no problem hiring me, but I needed to go through three more interviews before a final decision would be made. The first one would be with a psychologist that worked for the company, the second one with someone higher up in the company, and then the third one with another psychologist who was a former drug addict with thirty years of sobriety. He explained that even if I got hired, it would only be part-time and after thirty days, I would have to go through yet another interview with the owner himself, and he would determine if I would become a full-time counselor. I left there feeling good and was hopeful of getting hired, but knowing there was a final interview with the owner in order to become a full-time counselor did worry me a bit. I tried not to think about that, though, and focused on believing I would do well in all the other interviews first, and at least get hired. I was told, however, that these interviews would take quite some time to set up and take place, and to be patient as I waited.

As October was passing by, I would go to AA meetings and continue reading books about God, and I soon started thinking about doing something that I had wanted to do since I first got sober, which was to box again. I had been to a nearby gym with my wife to see some boxing matches in my first year sober because I had been thinking about boxing again at that time, but after the "treadmill incident," although I eventually started working out again, boxing remained nothing more than just a dream. Now, however, the idea of doing so started to consume me. I had been working out for some time at a gym my wife and I belonged to, and had gotten into very good shape by lifting weights and jogging, but I had also been hitting a hundred pound punching bag and jumping rope. Doing those two things put the idea in my head that with some more training, maybe I could actually have one more boxing match.

I was actually afraid to go to the boxing gym at first, but after two weeks of contemplation and daydreaming about boxing again, I finally got up enough nerve and went. After only a month of hitting the various punching bags, jumping more rope, and shadow boxing, I lost over ten pounds and at a hundred and fifty eight pounds, the dream of boxing again was now much more of a reality. I even began thinking about entering a seniors' tournament that would be held the following spring, and although this was for men in there early thirties and I would be turning forty-four years old the following month, I still fantasized about entering it and winning. I know this sounds crazy, but at the time, with the uncertainty I was feeling about getting the job as a counselor, I needed this dream. This dream also drove me to begin sparring with a few different boxers, and although I was afraid every time and because of this got tired very quickly, I eventually became less afraid and started to hold my own pretty well.

After only a few weeks of sparring, however, my dream of boxing again would soon end. It began one evening in early December while sparring with a much younger and stronger man than myself, but who was also less experienced. We were in the third and final round of our sparring and I had been talking to him through each round in an effort to help him with any mistakes he was making. Near the end of this particular round, however, it was me who made a mistake after I thought I was farther away from him than what I was. Just as I began to say something to him, he threw a punch that I thought would fall short but didn't. Although it wasn't a hard punch and only caught me on the very tip of my chin, my mouth was open at the time and the impact sent a burning sensation up through my jaw muscles. For a few seconds, I felt scared as I wondered how bad my jaw may be hurt, but this fear was replaced by something I had never felt before while sparring, which was anger. I had learned when I first began boxing how important it was to keep a cool head while in the ring, but now I didn't care and moved forward, throwing a few left-handed jabs with the intent of hitting him with a right hand. For some reason, though, I never threw the right hand, and a few seconds later, the bell rang to end the round.

I immediately got out of the ring to see how bad my jaw was hurt, and after getting my gloves off, I removed my mouthpiece; I could barely move my jaw at first. After opening and closing my mouth a few times, it felt a little better, but I knew my right jaw muscles were injured. I stood there moving my jaw around thinking how unbelievable it was that this had happened and at the same time hoping it wasn't bad enough to have to go to the doctor's. Still being unemployed and waiting for another interview at the detention home, I was actually more worried about this injury costing me money than how bad it may be, and remember laughing to myself for thinking this way.

When I got home that night, I was barely able to chew the bites of a sandwich I was trying to eat as I told my wife about what happened, and although she also laughed about me being worried if the injury would cost me money, she also expressed her concerns about me boxing again. This concern would go away that night after I realized even more of just how much of a different person I had become. After telling her how I didn't throw another punch at the young man, I realized that it was because I didn't want to hurt him—not that I really ever wanted to hurt someone while I was boxing; I knew it was part of the sport. Now here I was finally close to fulfilling my dream of boxing again, but the fact that I didn't want to hurt someone was telling me that it wasn't what I should be doing, and I knew that becoming a counselor for troubled teenagers was what I should be focusing on. Maybe the old Darryl needed to be a boxer to prove something to himself, but the one standing in the kitchen that night now knew in his heart that being a boxer was something he never truly wanted to be, and the dream of boxing again finally died that night.

As January rolled in and my money was running out, I decided while I was waiting to hear from the detention home that I would start working back at the electronics store I had left almost three years earlier. I had been stopping in since October, while waiting to hear from the detention home, to say hello to one of the guys I used to work with, and I got to know the new manager there pretty well. He would always ask me if I got the job as a counselor yet, and when I would say no, he would say that I should come back there to work again. Finally, one day in late November after stopping in and him asking me yet again to work there, still not having a job I said I wouldn't mind working there until I knew for sure I would get the job at the home, and he told me I could start in January after the holiday season was over. I was fortunate to be set up on an hourly pay instead of commission sales, because although I did sell some things while I was there, I didn't really have the old drive to sell like I used to. I did earn my keep, however, and over the next month and a half, I straightened up the whole store. I cleaned every inch of it I could first, including the restrooms, which were nasty, and then reorganized each showroom and added any new equipment that needed to be displayed. I then moved on to the warehouse and revamped that as well. I would also fight with my feelings of doubt and fear about not getting the job as a counselor by praying and then having hope that the interviews would soon happen. I also remember the idea of writing this book hitting me around this time, but after sitting down in one of the showrooms in the store and trying to write a few pages, I ended up ripping them up, and didn't think about it again.

By now it was February and I decided to call the program director to see if there was any news yet about my next interview. He told me he was just getting ready to call me because there would be one at the end of February, and as I wrote down the date, I was very excited. I was even more excited when the time came and during the interview, because of how long it had taken for it to happen, the psychologist who was interviewing me was kind enough to get me the next one that same day. I had to believe that this wasn't a coincidence because the person just happened to be at the detention home that day and was getting ready to leave when he got the call. Although he was an important person within the company, he was very down-to-earth and just like in the earlier interview, I did very well. It would take another month before I would have my last interview, and after doing well in that one too, I was finally hired on April 12th 2004 as a counselor's assistant. Even though this would be considered a part-time job, since I would still be working 36 hours a week over the different shifts there, I would need to quit working at the electronics store for a second time in my life. I would also reach my eighth year anniversary sober that month and celebrate the fact at another speaker's meeting, where I would share like I had the year before.

This time, however, not only was my wife there, but my daughter too, and it made it much more emotional for me than at any other time before. I would tell my story like I always did, but when I got to the part about when my daughter was born and how because of my drinking I didn't spend as much time with her as I wish I would have, I had to stop a few times because I was crying. Then when I got to the part about how when my daughter was little she was a daddy's girl, but that as she grew older this changed because of my alcoholism, I began crying much harder and had to stop again for a few moments until I regained enough composure to say how sorry I was for this, and how even today I still regret not spending more time with her and her brother. As I continued crying while telling everyone about the arguments she and her brother heard between my wife and me as they were growing up and about the toll this took on them and my wife, other people started crying too, including my wife and daughter. A little bit later I was able to stop crying long enough to explain just how the neglect and the arguments had affected her and my relationship, and how she didn't begin to fully realize the damage done by my drinking until after she turned eighteen and moved out.

I also explained how it took her almost five years to come to terms with what she went through growing up and to finally forgive me. I then shared that today our relationship was good and because of this that belief had become a very important part of my life over the last year. First I told them how believing in The Twelve Steps not only helped me stay sober, but change as a person, and that it was this change in myself that helped me to believe there had to be something that created the universe and life for a reason. I then told everyone that I call this something "God," and that I pray to it in the shower. I told them another reason why I believed this was because of a poem that my daughter had written for me the previous Christmas and how much it meant to me. As I read the poem, I began crying again as I said that even though she may never be a daddy's girl again, that it was because of this poem that I knew she loved me and had indeed forgiven me..

> If you taught me just one thing
> It is to love with all you have
> But you taught me so much more
> Through the good times and the bad

You showed me how to feel
Or at least passed this along
Even when I felt pain
You taught me to hold on

You proved that anyone can change
If you look within yourself
Even if you are feeling lonely
There is no need for someone else

You see the good in people
And have no tolerance for hate
I keep this in mind wherever I go
Even if I am always late

Genes have given me your sense of humor
I am goofy just like you
But you have made me realize
I can laugh at myself, too

There is no shame in crying
But self-pity is a waste of time
You and I have learned together
The power of the mind

You encourage me to believe
In more than just this life
Even when things look all gray
I know it will soon be all right

You are aware of your past
And have learned from your mistakes
You have taken your weaknesses
And turned them into strengths

You have shown me how to face your fears
And always tell the truth
Everyday heroes do exist
And you are living proof

The times when you thought you had failed
The times when you didn't know what to do
These are the moments you had no idea
That I would learn so much from you

I cried through the whole reading and when I was finished, I added how grateful I was for everything in my life today and ended by thanking everyone for being there. After that, a few other people told me how much they enjoyed hearing what I shared. The chips were handed out to other people who were also celebrating anniversaries, and when this was over, I received my chip for being sober eight years, which would mean more to me than all the others because of my daughter being there. Then with the meeting officially over, quite a few people came up to me to let me know how much what I had shared touched them and most also gave me a hug. This would bring tears to my eyes once again, and it wasn't until later that day that I realized how drained I was from the emotions I had at the AA meeting. I felt good, though, the rest of the day, and knowing I had the job at the detention home made me feel even better.

Feeling good about my job would continue over the next several weeks, but fears and insecurities would also surface, and after my interview with the owner took place in June, I would feel even more uncertain. I had already been introduced to him some time ago by the psychologist who interviewed me the last time, and he had struck me as a very mild mannered and likeable person. This time, however, even before the interview began, I could sense something was different about his demeanor when after introducing myself to him again and shaking his hand, he seemed very stern while telling me to have seat in front of his desk.

Although this made me feel a little more nervous than what I already was, I didn't think too much about it again until after I had answered a few preliminary questions. The first few were easy to answer, but then in a very serious and matter-of-fact manner he asked how I planned on making his teenagers feel safe and secure there in his facility. As I sat and thought about this, it must have been taking longer than he liked for me to answer because he again asked me how I was going to make his teenagers feel safe and secure. This time I answered right away and told him by gaining their trust in me.

He then flashed what I thought was a condescending smile, and I wasn't sure if it was a good answer or not. This made me begin to feel like I wasn't doing very well in the interview, and so I decided I would try to appear more confident with the next question. Unfortunately, this only seemed to make things worse, and with each question he seemed to be acting more and more resistant to me. Finally, however, the interview would take a turn for the better after he asked me how qualified I was for the job, considering I was going from being a salesman to working with teenagers. That's when I looked him straight in the eyes and told him that I would answer that question like I had in all the other interviews, but added that I would become emotional as I did so because of the passion I felt about helping others.

Since he knew I was a recovering alcoholic, I started out telling him that because of The Twelve Steps, I had learned many things that not only helped me to stop drinking, but enabled me to change the things about myself that made me want to drink in the first place. I then explained to him how in trying to become a better person than I was before for over eight years now, I had overcome many of my fears and insecurities and no longer dwelled so much in my negative emotions. I also told him that by seeing so many alcoholics who had gone through far worse circumstances than I did change and become well—and helping many of them myself—I had gained the confidence to believe I could help teenagers do the same thing. I went on to explain how I believed that telling someone about your own life and how you overcame the emotional troubles that caused you so much pain helped them to trust you enough to feel they could open up and talk to you about their own lives. Then, knowing he was a religious man, although I didn't go into my own beliefs, I did tell him that because I believed in God, it helped me believe I was meant to be here at this point in my life hoping to become a counselor.

After all this, I felt a change in him that I know came from my honesty, and he became friendlier. As we finished up the interview, I thought for sure I did well enough for him to hire me full-time, but he didn't. Instead, he told me as long as the good reports kept coming from the program director at the home, he would most likely hire me full-time around July or August. I felt very disappointed, which I think showed a little, but I tried to remain as composed as I could while sitting there. Finally, when we were through, I thanked him for the opportunity and said goodbye, but just like at the college earlier that year, I was once again leaving a place feeling sad and wondering why things didn't turn out the way I wanted them to. This time, however, although I would cry on the way home like I had after leaving the college, I wouldn't feel the despair like I had that day, and over the next few months I'd try to maintain the hope of becoming a full-time counselor. However, when July and August and even September passed by and it still didn't happen, I would search again for reassurance there was a God, and this time not only would I believe even more in a creator, but I would start believing in myself as well.

10

Why I Believe in a Creator and Myself

The only thing that I have found that helps me with my fear is faith. Faith there is something rather than nothing that created the universe and life for a reason. I call it God. And I pray to it in the shower. Several months have passed since I wrote the introduction to this book, and although I believe in myself even more now, I still turn to God whenever I need reassurance in my life that everything's going to be all right. I do this by simply asking God for the knowledge of its will and the power to carry it out, and for its wisdom and guidance. I then go on to thank God for everything in my life, and actually tell God I'm going to enjoy my day, be happy, and not worry about anything. Finally I finish by also telling God I love it, and that I know everything will be all right. The words may vary from time to time, but this is how I pray whenever fear enters my life and makes me unhappy. Fear that I have because of doubt. Doubt that when things aren't going well in my life, they won't change for the better. And doubt that faith in God will help me get through it.

I found out early on while working at the detention home, that although the Twelve Steps of Alcoholics Anonymous had helped me to grow spiritually and enable me to face many of the fears and insecurities I had in my life, they hadn't helped me grow enough in the kind of self confidence that I needed to face the ones I was experiencing there. These fears and insecurities were mainly due to the fact that most of the fifteen teenagers that resided at the home didn't seem to respond to my open and friendly nature and wouldn't listen to me in a group, but some of them came from the fact that I didn't feel accepted by a few of the counselors there. I found out later that the reason the teenagers, who were 13-17 year olds didn't respond to me was because they had trust issues. Some of these young men had suffered through different types of abuse, while some were abandoned by their fathers or had parents that simply didn't care about them, and the list goes on. The reason some of the counselors didn't take to me right away, however, was because they had learned to shut off their emotions so they wouldn't be affected by the hurtful behaviors displayed by some of the teens, or allow themselves to get too close to the ones they helped that would be released from the home someday.

Although I understood all of this, the combination of the way the teens and the counselors acted towards me filled me with a lot of doubts in myself early on, and there were times I wasn't sure I was cut out to be a counselor. Fortunately, because I had learned to deal with my fears and insecurities, I was able to get through those early months and by the end of September, I started to have more confidence. By the time October came and went, though, I still hadn't heard anything about being hired on as a full-time counselor. I again searched for reassurance there was something that created this life and the universe for a reason and this time not only did I see more than ever a design to this world and that something had to have created it, but I also began to believe more in the possibility we could create our lives the way we wanted them to be through our thoughts and beliefs.

That's why in November I stopped dreaming of becoming a full-time counselor and started writing the introduction to my book. I wasn't sure where to start, but by January of 2005, I had finished the introduction and let some of the counselors at the detention home read it to see what they thought. They all liked it and one of them who could still be standoffish towards me, actually told me not to change anything because it was good. This helped to boost my confidence in being able to write my book, and although there were times when my fears and insecurities would still surface while working there, I also had enough confidence to handle the teenagers by myself now. It was while they were in their rooms that this could sometimes be the most challenging, and I had to learn very quickly how to handle many different situations. There were six rooms in the upstairs part of the farmhouse and two bathrooms for the teenagers to use. These rooms weren't very large, but they were big enough to put as many as three beds in them and there were always two to three teens in each room. One room was called the security room because it was the one where the new arrivals stayed until they could be trusted more, and was the one I had to keep my eye on the most. I would sit by the doorway where I had full view of the room and so they could also see me, but I occasionally had to get up and check on some of the teens in the other rooms too.

There were also times when I had to address questions from some of the teens who would first ask to "step to the door." This was what the teens were supposed to say to come to their doors if there was something important they needed to ask about, but it was almost always something silly and quite the opposite. I loved being up there and having fun with them, and it was hard to remember that some of them had done some very awful things in their lives. This never bothered me, though, because I knew people in AA who had done terrible things and changed for the better and I believed these young men could do the same. There were times, however, when disagreements between the teens would happen and need to be quickly addressed so they didn't escalate, but I had learned how to handle these situations from the counselors there. I had also learned a lot from them about why these teens showed the different types of behaviors they did, which helped me know how to handle the difficult situations that would sometimes arise. There were those times, however, when a threat of some kind of punishment had to be made if they didn't stop whatever they were doing wrong. I didn't like having to threaten them and tried my best to reason with the teens first, but sometimes I would put on the tough guy shoes and let them know their behaviors were unacceptable and they needed to stop. I saw this work with the counselors that really were tough guys, and although it did frighten most of them enough to listen, there were still times when one of them would become threatening enough that a physical encounter called a "restraint" couldn't be avoided. I hated when this happened, because it involved some of the counselors holding down a teenager until they were calm and acknowledged they would listen. Thankfully I never had to be involved in one of these.

I was, however, involved in a physical encounter with one of the teens in February that would have a lasting effect on both me and the teenagers. I got to work that morning at the required time—fifteen minutes before the first shift began. I loved working this shift, because I got to spend the day with the teenagers at the school they went to that sat across from the detention home. It wasn't very large, but could comfortably hold at least twenty-five people if necessary. There were two teachers that taught them everything from History to Algebra, and I would try and help the teenagers with some of their work and keep them in line during the time they were there. Before school started that day, however, I would learn that I no longer wanted to play the tough guy.

I walked into the small, elongated room that morning where the teenagers gathered after getting up, groomed, and dressed for the day and, for security reasons, sat down beside a table near the only door as I always did. I hadn't slept well the night before, so instead of mingling with them as I usually did, I just sat there watching them. They were a mixed group of mostly whites, some blacks, and a few were mixed from having parents of both races, but none seemed to care as they sat in a semi-circle on stackable chairs and talked with each other or watched the Sports News Show on a 36-inch TV. One young man in particular, however, who, at 6'1 and 200-plus pounds, could be called the leader of the group, would often act up in this setting, and that morning was no exception. He was well aware that his behaviors influenced the other teenagers and before I could even take a sip of the coffee I had brought along to wake me up, he got up out of his seat without asking and approached me. I asked him what he wanted and when it became evident he only wanted to agitate me like he was known for doing to the other teenagers and most of the counselors, I told him to just sit down and relax. He did, but then started picking on some of the other teens by saying dumb things he knew would offend them, and although I had learned to be patient, as these types of behaviors were common not just for him but for some of the other teens as well, when he persisted in disrupting the whole group, I finally told him he needed to stop it now. That's when he got up and walked around me and put me in a choke hold.

I had trusted him enough to allow him to walk behind me and even after he did this, I still told him nicer than I felt I should have to please stop it and go sit down. By now, the whole group had started watching this, and I knew I was in a tough situation as far as keeping the respect I had from the other teenagers, so I told him once again but with more authority to let go of me and sit down. When he didn't and his hold on me grew even tighter, I took off the glasses I occasionally wore and as I laid them down, I told him if he didn't let go of me and sit down I would make him. I had really only said this as an attempt to intimidate him, but when it didn't work, I knew I would now have to carry out my threat. I did this by quickly standing up, and although he was able to maintain his hold because he was three inches taller than me, it wasn't as strong as before, and I was able to eventually work my way free and turn around to face him. I somehow managed to wrestle him to the floor and sit on his chest while pinning his arms down on either side of his head.

Although he would struggle and almost throw me off a few times, when he finally settled down a little, just to make sure he knew to never challenge me again, I let go of his arms and quickly but lightly slapped him on either side of his face while asking him, "Are you ready to stop now?" This wasn't hard enough to hurt him and was really only meant to show him and the other teenagers that I could handle him, but it turned out to be a big mistake. Some of them began yelling things that included, "The old man got you!" and I could see it angered him. Still, because he didn't really struggle, I thought maybe he was embarrassed enough to indeed want to stop, and so I decided to let him go. As I began to stand up, however, he used his legs like a gigantic pair of scissors and wrapped them around mine, making me fall to the floor. This angered me and I immediately jumped to my feet with nothing hurt except my pride, but as fast as I got up, he was already standing there facing me. This was when the counselor on duty asked if I wanted some help, but with my pride hurt from the fall I said no and proceeded to grab the teenager by his arms and began backing him up. I believe the young man may have no longer wanted to continue as he felt he had redeemed himself by making me fall and didn't want to risk any further embarrassment, but I was too wrapped up in making sure he knew who the boss was, and what happened next could have been avoided.

As I was backing him up, we somehow turned to my left and away from the closet door that was behind us and ended up going backwards four or five feet until I was holding him against a different closet door. It was here that he broke free, but I grabbed his arms again and pushed him back against the closet door to let him know, once again, I was in control. As we stood there looking at each other for a few seconds, I could feel the tension leave us and as we both started to smile I let go of his arms, but when I did, he playfully tried to see if I was fast enough to stop him from getting away by moving quickly to his right away from the door. I was fast enough the first time he did this and caught him and held him there again, and realizing he was now making a game of this, I let him go and waited for him to try again. This time, however, when he moved and I went to grab his arms to push him back like before, I missed altogether and hit my forehead on the door. It was after this that I finally gave some ground and said to him sarcastically, but with a smile "There. Are you happy now? I hit my head, now go sit down." and when he smiled back, I knew he would.

When I turned away from the closet door, however, I felt a warm trickle run down the right side of my nose and the counselor who had offered help wasn't smiling when he said to me, "You need to go to the restroom." I thought this warm trickle was blood coming from the area where I had hit my head, but because it didn't hurt I simply thought it was probably just a slight break in the skin. When I got to the restroom, however, and looked into one of the two mirrors that hung above the sinks, there was a lot more blood running down by my entire face. It was coming from a hole the size of a pea to the right of my left eyebrow just above where the bridge of my nose started. Although I wasn't sure how it got there, I knew I had to stop the flow of blood and put some ice on it. I would find out later that the gash was from a one-inch square steel latch that stuck out on the closet door that had a hole in it for a lock to fit into that we used to secure the teens' jackets. All I could think about for the moment was getting some ice for my injury and cleaning up the blood that was all over my face and neck now, and even on the restroom floor.

After wrapping an ice pack in some paper towels, I put it against my forehead where the hole was and went back into the restroom and began washing my face and neck off with the paper towels from the dispenser. When I finished doing that, I threw the blood-stained towels into the garbage can, got some more, and bent down and cleaned the floor up as well. Finally, when I was through with all of this, I remember standing there in the restroom looking at myself in the mirror with the paper towel-covered ice pack between my eyes, and with a half-smile on my face, wondered what reason there could for this to happen in my life now. There would be a phone call to the owner about what happened and the program director himself would give the teen a thorough talking to about the incident to once again try and make him understand that these types of behaviors had to stop. This teen had been responsible for hurting two other counselors in the past, and while I was basically responsible for my own injury, the teen had to understand it wouldn't have happened if he had listened to me. After that, I would go to the hospital and receive six stitches to close up the hole and the half-inch cuts above and below it, but not before I would play the tough guy for the last time in my life.

After everything had settled down, as I was waiting for one of the teachers to drive me to the hospital, as a joke, I walked into the room and removed the ice bag I was holding on my wound, and said to them. "Who's next?" They looked at me almost in disbelief as I stood there looking around the room at all of them pretending to mean this with this hole in my head and blood still running down and I heard one of them say, "Duke's crazy," but once I smiled, they knew I was just having fun. Although this initially fed what was left of my false sense of ego, and I would go on for the next week or so feeling some pride in being able to handle myself as well as I did against a bigger and stronger teenager, both my false sense of ego and the tough guy act would die the next day. I came to work in the morning and the teens were already done eating their breakfast and were sitting in the small, oblong room as usual. This was also the room used for their daily morning sessions that were held by whatever counselor was in charge that day, and for various group sessions held by the program director or supervisor that I had the fortune of sitting in on and occasionally participating in.

This morning, however, the supervisor was already in there talking to the teens about what happened the day before, and as I walked in and took my usual seat by the door, all the teens looked over at me. After a short time, the supervisor finished up talking to the teens and then asked if there was anything I wanted to add. I had not yet reached the confidence that the other counselors seemed to have while speaking to the group, and so I was a little nervous, but this would quickly change. I first looked around the room at all the young men who, while at other times, hadn't always given me their undivided attention, now sat there quietly staring at me and waiting to hear what I had to say. After this, I proceeded to speak to them about the day before in the only way I knew how, which was with the type of openness and honesty that I had been told over four years ago was the language of the heart. I first told them how I never again

118

wanted to go through that with any of them, because it wasn't who I wanted to be. Then even though they had all heard my life story before, I again went over how I had always tried to be something I wasn't in order to feel better about myself. After that, I told them that I had put on the "tough guy" shoes yesterday and they no longer fit me. I explained by doing what I did yesterday, although it made me feel good about myself to play the tough guy, I didn't feel good about myself now. Then as I added that I cared about and truly loved each and every one of them, I started to cry and had to stop briefly. When I was able to continue, I told them that while the teen shouldn't have put me in a chokehold like he did, what happened afterwards was my fault because of me trying to be something I wasn't.

I looked around the room and thought of what I wanted to say to them next, and I saw how every one of these young men were looking at me with an attentiveness I had never seen them display before as a group. This prompted me to tell them how I didn't care about the things they did in the past and how I believed in my heart that each one of them was capable of being a better person. I told them to believe me when I say that I love you guys and care about you, and that I'm not afraid to sit here and say this or ashamed to cry in front of you, because this is who I really am. There was dead silence in the room for several seconds, and I remember making some kind of joke to lighten things up. Then, like when I spoke at my AA Anniversary Meetings and people would comment afterwards about some of the things I had shared, many of the teenagers also began to comment on what I had just said to them. This made me feel like I had finally been able to reach them as a group, but when a few of them would add, "and we love you too, Duke," to what they had said, I knew I had reached some of them in a way no one else had.

From that day on, I had very few problems with any of the young men and I believe this was because they knew I really did love and care about them. I would, however, still experience some differences with a couple of the counselors there, but this would only strengthen the now growing belief in myself, and eventually even these counselors would realize I really was the person I said I was in the first chapter of this book—someone who had become happy with himself by trying hard to be a good person and is full of love for himself and others. And someone who is honest about his emotions and not afraid to talk about them, or ashamed to cry because of them. But more importantly, that I was now, more than anything else, someone who wanted to tell the world how a search for reassurance in some kind of God helped to change my beliefs about life, and inspired me to write this book.

Sadly, however, by July of that year, I would leave the detention home to do just that by working part-time with teenagers in a Big Brothers-like program, and although I enjoyed it and cared about every new teenager I met, I would often miss the ones I met at the detention home. I did, however, try to apply many of the things I had learned from the counselors there to help these new teenagers, and I would especially use some of the knowledge I had obtained from the program director. I had learned a lot from him by sitting in group sessions and listening to him speak to the teenagers, and I am not ashamed to say that he also helped me learn a lot about myself. Although he was hard on me at times, I know it was to help me in my quest to be a good counselor and a stronger person. He simply saw in me the qualities it took to be a good counselor, but also knew what my weaknesses were, and did his best to help me get rid of them. If he wouldn't have pushed me to the limits he did, I may never have realized what my true capabilities were and grow to the level of confidence in myself that I did. He also helped me become a wiser person in the many talks we had in the kitchen of that old farmhouse after my shift ended.

It was there that we would have discussions on many different subjects and I would listen attentively to his views on politics and his perspective on racism as a black person. My favorite discussions, however, were about the behaviors of emotionally troubled teenagers and adults. Oftentimes, I found myself agreeing with the things he said that were taken from his years of experience in this field, and it slowly helped me build a confidence that I knew more than I thought I did. There were a couple of times, however, that I would find myself disagreeing with him, but he didn't seem to care and displayed an air of confidence in himself that he was right, which would take me awhile longer to achieve. Nevertheless, I gained a lot of knowledge from these talks and learned more from him and working at the detention home than any college classes could ever have taught me. When I first began working at the Big Brothers-like organization, however, I soon discovered that I felt a little uncomfortable when I was one-on-one with teenagers. This basically stemmed from never having learned how to form a friendship with anyone, and there were some quiet moments when I was with them. Of course I had learned at the detention home how to relate to teenagers and had conversations with them about things other than their behaviors and emotions, but these were short conversations and usually only after they began trusting me and opening up to me. By having only one or two teens over a four-hour period, I first had to find a way to get them to open up enough to even tell me a few things about themselves, and even when they did, it was hard for me to keep finding things to talk about with them. It was through these early experiences, however, that I learned how to relate even better to teenagers, and as time went on, I had no trouble getting most of the new teens I was assigned to talk to me and even have fun with them.

I was having some troubles in my personal life though. Since the beginning of the year, a noticeable tension between my wife and I had been building, and although I wasn't sure why it was happening, I did think it was more her then me. This tension became even more apparent on one occasion in July and involved my daughter, who was seven months pregnant at the time. In 2003, she had fallen in love with a handsome and very tall young man who was a year younger than her at only 22 years of age, and someone my wife and I would learn to care very much for. From day one he seemed like a perfect fit for my daughter, who depending on how you looked at it, was either fortunate or unfortunate to have inherited my personality, as he was very laid back and let my daughter be who she was. He was also the one who helped share the news back in January of this year that my wife and I would be grandparents. Anyway, we had set out that day to go visit our daughter at the apartment she and this young man shared, and after a stop along the way to pick something up for her at a pharmacy, we got into a small argument over something I can barely remember now. Unfortunately, what could have been a short-lived argument didn't end after we got to the apartment.

Everything seemed fine when we first got there as my wife and I hugged and kissed our daughter, but both of us were noticeably quiet. As my wife and daughter sat down in the little dining area in her apartment and started chatting, I walked into the small walk-in kitchen area beside it and started to clean up some dishes in the sink. It didn't take long for my daughter to realize something was wrong, however, and she asked my wife about it. She immediately started crying as she told my daughter about the tension we were experiencing and how she felt I wasn't being nice to her, and this infuriated me. I had worked hard to improve on my relationship with my daughter over the years and I didn't want what my wife was saying to hurt that, plus I truly felt it was more my wife's behaviors than my own that led to our arguments. It also infuriated my daughter, because I no sooner walked over to try and tell my side of the story, when my daughter, who was already hugging her crying mother, looked at me and told me to leave. I couldn't believe what I was hearing and tried to explain how this wasn't all my fault, but between my daughter being tired from her pregnancy and having also inherited my old temper, I never got the chance. First, she blamed me for coming over there and doing this with her being pregnant, and then told me once again to get out, but this time she was swearing and much louder. I tried my best to reason with her about why this wasn't fair, but I slowly began to see that it was no use. Not only was her fatigue and temper causing her to lash out at me, but also all the painful memories she had from living at home of me starting fights and upsetting her mother.

This day was a terrible reminder for me of just how devastating it was for my daughter to grow up with an alcoholic father, but some good did come out of it. I spent the next two days searching for a reason why this happened and as angry and hurt as I had been, I began to realize I could move through something like this and still grow from it. I went over to my daughter's that same week to talk to her about what happened, and when she answered the door, she seemed happy to see me and told me to come in. After going inside the apartment and shutting the door, I immediately started the conversation by making some kind of joke about what had happened and it made her laugh. It also prompted her to explain that it was her hormones being out of whack that caused her to act the way she did. I was the one who apologized for the whole thing, however, and then went on to explain to her that I felt it was the memories she had of how I used to be that caused her behaviors. She disagreed with me, but because I knew better, I didn't force the issue. I did, however, begin to cry as I promised to be a better grandpa than I was a dad. This made her cry as well, and as we then hugged each other she told me, "It's all right Dad, I love you." I would leave that day without being asked to this time, feeling much better about our relationship, but the tension between me and wife would remain.

She and I did share a very nice experience together the following month, though, when she went along with me to see the teenagers at the detention home on Labor Day. I remember I was no sooner out of the car when I was greeted by the teens who were outside having a cook-out; they ran up to me with smiles on their faces yelling, "Duke! Duke!" It filled me with pride when they did this and warmed my heart to know they had apparently missed me as much as I did them, and after giving each one a hug and finding out a few of them were a little sweaty, I introduced them all to my wife. They liked this and were quite respectful towards her as I introduced each one by name, but as most of them were known to do, when I was done, their attention quickly shifted to something else. They had just finished painting these large rocks they had collected and wanted to show them to me, while a few of them wanted to show me other things they did that day. It was after this that I realized a couple of the teens were down at a garden they had started in the spring, so I walked down to talk to them as well. They were also very happy to see me, and after a few minutes of talking with them, one of them introduced me to some new teenagers that had arrived after I left.

This whole experience had been quite emotional for me, and when it came time for my wife and I to leave, I choked up a little bit as I was saying goodbye to all of them. This then prompted one of the teens to say, "Duke's going to cry," and as I hugged every one of them before I left, I didn't care one bit that I had tears in my eyes or that some of them were still sweaty. That day gave even more confidence that I had been right to tell these teenagers who I was and not be afraid to express my feelings of love for them, and I would continue to do this with the ones at the Big Brothers-like organization.

There was another experience that month that my wife and I shared together that nothing could ever compare to, which was the arrival of our grandchild. This was by far the best day I ever had in my sobriety and there was no tension between my wife and me that day at all. She was actually with my daughter and her husband the whole time including the birth, and only ten minutes later I got to see the little boy my daughter brought into this world, and when I saw him for the first time, I cried as I stood and stared at the little bundle of joy that was now my grandchild.

I must confess that at this point in my life, while crying at moments like this certainly didn't bother me, the whole crying thing in general had begun to concern me a little. Over the last two months, I had not only started crying more when sharing at AA meetings, but in my personal life as well, and it didn't seem to matter where I was or who I was talking to when I did. I could be in my car talking to the teens I was working with, at the home of a friend or relative, or even in a mall talking to a complete stranger. It did, however, matter what I was talking about when it happened. I would cry at different moments when talking about my past or the spiritual growth I had experienced throughout my sobriety, and especially when I talked about the various beliefs I now held that made me want to help others. While most people I talked to didn't seem to mind this and would actually agree with many of the things I said I believed in, crying while talking to people not only worried me, but also made me start to think I may be going crazy. I remember more than a few times while sitting at my computer and writing my book, stopping and wondering exactly what it was I was feeling, and what I was going through.

Thankfully, sometime in September, through what I believe was another non-coincidence, I would find out from someone what it was I may be going through. I was at a gym with a couple of my teenagers and as they seemed contented going from machine to machine and not acting up, I started to talk to someone who was working out there. It turned out he was a college student and we talked about a few different things including politics, and after I told him I was writing a book and what it was about, he shared that he too believed in some type of creator. Because of this, I felt compelled to also tell him about my recent behaviors and how I was feeling because of them. He said that it sounded like I was experiencing something called self-actualization, but at the time I didn't think anything about it, and after talking a little bit more with him, before we said our goodbyes I told him how much I appreciated talking with him.

Later that night, I decided to look self-actualization up on the Internet, and although there is a lot written on the subject, I feel what a professor named Abraham Maslow wrote in an article called, "A Theory of Human Motivation" best describes it. He defines self-actualization to be "the desire for self-fulfillment, namely the tendency for the person to become actualized in what he is potentially. This tendency might be phrased as the desire to become more and more what one is and to become everything that one is capable of becoming." He used the term self-actualization to describe a desire, not a driving force, which could lead to realizing one's capabilities. He didn't feel that self-actualization determined one's life; rather, he felt that it gave the individual a desire, or motivation to achieve budding ambitions. After reading this and many other writings on self-actualization, I began to believe this was exactly what I was going through. It simply made so much sense to me because of how I had been continually trying to grow both spiritually and as a person, and I immediately felt like a weight had been lifted off of my shoulders, and that I wasn't going crazy after all.

Despite this, there would still be times when I didn't feel like I was growing spiritually because of some of the things I did, and I would get mad at myself for it. One of these things was that I could sometimes hurt people when trying to be "the funny guy." I never really thought I needed to change this part of me because most people seemed to enjoy my humor, but in October it became apparent that I needed to be more aware of what I said when joking around with certain people. My wife and I had gone to a small get-together that month at her sister and brother-in-law's place, and later that night I made a joke about someone there. The person who I made the joke about wasn't actually there to hear me and at the time I honestly didn't think that much about it, but I remember before going to sleep that night thinking maybe I shouldn't have made the joke. It was the next day that I really wish I hadn't made the joke because my wife's brother-in-law called me that morning, upset about it. Apparently, someone who was this person's friend didn't appreciate what I said, and it upset them that I would say what I did even jokingly. He also told me that while he personally liked my sometimes over the edge type of humor, not everyone did, and that this wasn't the first time I upset someone or hurt their feelings by joking around. I felt very bad about this and started to cry as I told him how I used to do this in my drinking days and that because of this I certainly didn't want to do it now. I added that I honestly hadn't been aware that I was doing this and how sorry I was for it.

He tried to make me feel better by telling me he told the person that I'm a good person and that he knows I didn't mean to hurt anyone, and I told him how much I thought of him and that I appreciated him making me aware of this as it would help me stop doing it. Although it was hard for me to accept what I heard, as I mentioned earlier, a part of spiritual growth is knowing you will always need to keep growing and this experience would help me do just that.

The rest of the year ran smoothly for me as I enjoyed visiting my grandchild and kept plugging away at my book, but the tension would continue between me and my wife and slowly become worse the following year. It seemed no matter what I said, she disagreed, and this affected more than just our personal relationship. Our sex life had slowly been dropping off over the last few years and by 2006, it was anything but passionate, and I often felt she was only doing it because she felt she had to. This upset me because I had worked hard to overcome the damage my drinking had done in this department. In all fairness, my wife had been going through menopause for some time, which I knew affected her sex drive, but between the tension in our relationship and the lack of sex, I could be quite resentful towards her at times and not be very spiritual.

This lack of spirituality affected the progress of my book, as I didn't feel very inspired to write, and I soon found a new reason to distract me from writing. Back around the time my grandchild was born, I discovered there were different security software programs that protect your computer from viruses and things called spyware, and I would read about them on the Internet, then install them to try them out. Although at first it didn't seem like a problem, as my relationship with my wife slowly got worse, I started doing it more and more. By the middle of 2006, I even joined an online forum that enabled me to post back and forth with other people about these security programs. I soon became quite addicted to not only trying out different security programs, but also this forum, and would often stay up late at night reading posts and posting my thoughts about the various security software and then be too tired to write anything for my book the next day. This upset me and I would try to stop so it didn't interfere with my writing, but as the tension between me and my wife continued, so did my addiction, and there were days when it was hard to write, but I would try anyway. I would also continue my quest for spiritual and personal growth, but it wouldn't be easy.

Since the beginning of that year, my son, who was now twenty-two and still living at home, had slowly been showing his underlying anger towards me. I had actually thought everything was fine between us up until then because whenever I talked to him about the regrets I had of not being a good father or told him how sorry I was for not being with him more when he was growing up, he would tell me it was all right and that it didn't bother him. However, as the year progressed, this anger towards me grew worse. I began to see even more how the years of neglect he went through as a child had truly affected him. I tried to talk to him about it, but because he would get even angrier and clam up when I did, it quickly became apparent that I needed to back off and give him some time to work through what he was feeling. Thankfully, there were times when we did get along well enough to at least talk about his day, which helped the situation somewhat, but it still hurt that he wouldn't open up to me about his anger so I could help him with it.

Despite this and the tension between me and my wife, I would continue trying to grow more spiritual. Toward the end of summer, I decided that to better do this, I needed to stop joking around as much. I had been doing pretty well at watching who I joked around with, and as far as I knew hadn't upset anyone again, but I still felt it was interfering with my spiritual and personal growth. My wife had been pointing out for years that I joked around too much, but I always thought it was because she didn't share my sense of humor. It was hard trying not to be the "funny guy" and not joke around all the time, and I remember when I first decided to do this, it felt like I was losing an old friend. In a way I was, as being the "funny guy" had always helped me overlook my fears and insecurities, and there were still times when I would use my sense of humor to get through nerve-wracking situations. I also continued to try and work on my relationship with my son, but it become even more apparent near the end of the year that his anger towards me, and in general, was getting even worse. Although he wouldn't threaten me physically, he was now verbally attacking me at almost every opportunity, and it all came to a head in November.

Our argument began over something simple and esca-lated very quickly, ending with him telling me I was the worst father ever and that he wished I was dead. This hurt, but I knew it was a good thing that the anger he felt towards me was truly coming out. I remember calling my daughter, saying I believed my relationship with her brother was getting better now because he told me I was the worst father ever and that he wished I was dead. She started laughing, and as we talked more about what happened, she agreed it was a good sign. We had already talked about her brother's anger towards me several times that year and she was the one who had made me understand just how neglected he had really been as a child. As the conversation continued, I told her how he was also neglected as a teenager after I had stopped drinking. He was only a few months away from turning thirteen when I first got sober, and over the next several years, as I worked on becoming a better person than I was before, although I was showing him love and giving him some attention, I still wasn't doing the things a father needed to do to bond with his son. My daughter shared how she too had felt neglected by me as a child. This surprised me, because I had spent more time with her than I had her brother and when we had talked about her childhood before, she never mentioned it.

I think that by now having a child of her own and spending so much time with him, it made her realize how I had never spent the kind of time with either one of them that I should have. She also told me that she had told her brother that he needed to move out because of how it had helped her eventually get over her own anger towards me, and it wasn't long after our conversation that he actually did. It was in December around my birthday and he joked about it being a birthday present to me. Although I was glad he was moving out because I hoped it would indeed help our relationship, it still saddened me that he was leaving. On the day he left, I told him while crying, of course, that I loved him and as I hugged him, I promised our relationship would get better. He hugged me back and afterwards I could tell he was also a little emotional, and it made me feel good that he got that way.

I would leave the Big Brothers-like organization that month to work at a different one, but by now I had formed the opinion that programs like these weren't always the best avenue for some of the more troubled teenagers. This was mostly due to the various rules and regulations in place at these types of organizations that I felt didn't always give you the amount of time needed to gain the trust of some of the more troubled teenagers, or the authority to push them hard enough to get them to open up and talk to you. I usually only had 7.5 hours a week to spend with each of them, and had to be careful with some of the things I said and did with them. I still tried my best to help them understand and talk about their emotions, and not let myself get too frustrated when I couldn't reach them like I wanted to.

It's not that these organizations didn't help teenagers, but that they were businesses that needed to make money to stay open, and I felt this need to make money sometimes led to keeping the more emotionally troubled teenagers in the program instead of getting the level of help they needed. The entire juvenile system doesn't seem to have the funding needed to provide better training and better pay to the many workers involved in helping teenagers. Even though it's not only about the money, when people are overworked and underpaid, no matter how much they care, not every teenager is going to get the extra help they may need. Through these organizations, however, I was fortunate to meet some very nice people who cared as much about the teenagers they helped as I did.

December was also the month that I started thinking I may be able to finish writing my book soon. I had actually hoped to have it completed much sooner than this, but between the days when I'd struggle to convey in words the things I felt I needed to and the ones when I was either too tired to write or didn't feel inspired to, it just kept taking longer than I expected. By now, though, I had managed to have ten chapters done and with only two left to write, I was sure I could finally finish it and send it off to an editor by February. Knowing I would need a job afterwards, I even called one of the young ladies I used to work with at the cell phone company to see about working there again and when she told me they needed people and would most likely start hiring soon, it appeared everything was in place to finish my book and work there until it was published. Although I was very excited about finishing it, knowing how close I was to actually doing so filled me with more fears of its success.

I have to admit that by now money did play a small part in getting it finished and published because it was running out. From the time I had started working at the detention home up until now, I had used up what little bit of money I had in my savings, and over half of the money I took out of the two separate IRAs I had from when I worked at the electronics store and at the cell phone company. It wasn't a lot of money by some people's standards, I suppose, but it did total over $14,000 and it would seem all I had to show for it at this time was a dream and an unfinished book. It also became more apparent around this time that writing my book was what was causing some of the tension between me and wife. She had told me a few times that year how worried she was about our finances with me only working part-time, but she also had started claiming it was affecting my personality. She claimed I had changed since I began writing my book, and in an argument we had the month before, even claimed I was becoming more arrogant. I didn't see it that way, as I felt I had become much more humble over the years, but I did try my best to understand what she was going through.

I also kept trying to believe I could finally finish my book, and as January got underway, I began working toward that. About a week into it, however, something told me I needed to include the parts about the whole "Julia Roberts thing," and it ended up taking me almost two months to finish it. I got stuck many times while trying to explain what I was going through at that time in my life, and even when I was finally done, I still wasn't exactly sure what I had gone through back then. The delay in finishing it made me feel dejected. I tried to believe there was a reason for why I still hadn't finished my book, but when I called the girl I knew to see about a job, she told me they had just finished hiring all the people they needed, which made me feel more hopeless. Not only wasn't I finished with my book, but now I wasn't even going to get a job I thought for sure I would. It saddened me when she told me this, but with hardly any money left, I started looking for another one right away.

It actually didn't take long, as my wife found an opening listed in the local paper for a customer service rep at a large furniture store. I called to set up an interview, and to my surprise they asked me if I wanted to come in that same day. I really didn't want to, but with the scarcity of jobs at the time, I thought I better go. The interview was with the store manager and another young lady and it was quite extensive. I could tell from their reactions and their behaviors towards me I did very well in the interview, and the store manager told me he would put in a good word for me to help me get the position. Because the interview went so well, I felt confident that I had a good chance of getting the job, but I planned on staying at the Big Brothers-like organization until I knew for sure. Unfortunately, this didn't go quite as planned, as a few weeks later, I had an incident with someone on a disciplinary board for the teens on probation and had no choice but to quit. One of the people on this panel started to question one of my teens and accused him of lying about something he hadn't. I got upset and felt the need to defend him. Unfortunately, the organization I was working for did not defend me for doing my job—being an advocate for my teen. I left there that day upset and angry and when I started feeling very resentful, I called a friend I knew from AA to talk about it. This helped me to work through my anger and even laugh about losing my job, but the incident would bother me for several more days.

I also called the manager at the furniture store that day in hopes he had heard something about me getting the position there. Although he hadn't heard anything, he told me he would check and only a day later, he called me to say I got the job. I would first have a week of training in another store and in early April I would become a customer service rep for the second time in my life. I thought I was really going to like this job, as I had enjoyed doing customer service work at the cell phone store, but in just the first couple of days, my friendly and outgoing personality kept clashing with a few of the people there, including the manager of that department, and it quickly became apparent this job wasn't for me. I talked to the store manager about the situation and we both agreed that me staying there wasn't going to work out. I felt relieved I would be no longer working there.

But after waking up the next morning jobless and with no opportunities on the horizon, I started feeling depressed and anxious. I remember trying to fight these emotions by praying and telling my wife how I was feeling, but even playing with our grandchild who we babysat two days out the week didn't help. Even feeling this way, I tried as hard as I could to believe everything would be all right, and later that morning after receiving a phone call from the manager of the cell phone company I used to work for about a job, I began to believe things would work out. I had stopped in at the store on the same day I knew the job at the furniture store wasn't for me to tell the girl I used to work with about how I didn't like my new job and to see if one may be opening up there soon. Although she didn't say anything to me that day, she knew the company was planning on opening two new stores very soon, and told the manager I had stopped in and was still interested in working there. A few days later, the manager, who when I worked there was the "new employee trainer," told me that if I was definitely interested in working there, I should come in as soon as possible for what would amount to an informal interview and to get the paperwork out of the way so everything would be ready when one of the new stores opened. This was almost unbelievable to me, as I had thought getting a job there wasn't going to happen anytime soon, and after we set a day to meet, I thanked him for the opportunity and said goodbye. Only a few seconds later, I began to cry as the relief I felt from knowing I'd soon have a job overwhelmed me, and because I believed this had to be another of the many "non-coincidences" that have been a part of my sobriety.

After a few weeks, he called to let me know that I would start working in that store the following week until the new one opened up and that I would get a guaranteed income for the first two months to help take any pressures of selling off and also a sign-on bonus. When the new store finally opened up and I began working there, I was happy to be in a brand new, clean store. After the first few days went by, however, a familiar sadness started to come over me. I knew some of this was due to the fact that I really missed working with teenagers and I often had to tell myself that the job was only temporary and I'd be able to move on once my book was published. However, when this familiar sadness kept coming back, I knew there had to be a deeper meaning to it. I had plenty of time to figure out what I was going through, as this new store didn't have many customers yet, and I even talked to the guy I worked with about how I was feeling in hopes of getting to the bottom of it. Although we were two completely different people when it came to our politics and religion, we found it easy to talk and joke around with each other, and over time, we became very close friends.

Finally, after another week passed, one afternoon it suddenly hit me that by working here I didn't feel fulfilled in my life like I had working with teenagers and the reason the sadness felt so familiar was because it was the same sadness I felt through the "Julia Roberts thing." This was a revelation for me, because I had never been sure of what I had actually gone through at that time, but now I knew it was because I wasn't fulfilled in my life back then either or while working at the cell phone company the first time. There was one other thing I realized that day, which was the most important thing of all. Over this time, I hadn't felt the unimportance like I had back then and knew this was because I had grown much more confident and secure in myself, and was now happy with who I was. After discovering all this that day, I started to feel better and would rarely feel the sadness, but I would remain unfulfilled. One thing about growing as a person, however, is that as your interests and views on life change, you slowly become more aware of how other people haven't grown, and it was around this time that I began to see just how much this was adding to the tension between me and my wife. While I had been very dependent on my wife for many things, including my emotional stability, throughout my drinking days and much of my sobriety, by my eighth year sober I had become a lot more reliant on myself to be well, and I know this began to bother her.

She had always been the type of person to want to help people with problems in their lives, and she was still the one our children went to whenever they needed help in theirs. However, now that I had grown more in my self-confidence and no longer needed her help, she began to see this as arrogance on my part and evidence that I had changed. Obviously I had changed, but whenever I would try to explain to her that this arrogance was only self-confidence and nothing more, she just wouldn't see it that way. All I felt I could do about this was to try harder to get along with her and to love her unconditionally, but this was hard for me as I was just beginning to learn to love myself that way.

I remember one time she even accused me of acting like I did in my drinking days, and it started a big argument between us. If there was anything that still filled me with anger at this time, it was the idea that I was the same person I was when I was drinking. I had worked so hard to change over my sobriety and become a better person than I was before that I wasn't about to let anyone tell me I was the same as I was back then, especially someone that I felt hadn't grown like I had. Although no one else was accusing me of this, other family members started to see a difference in me as well. This was mostly because when I was around them, I would almost always talk about my book, and how I wanted to make a difference in the world, and eventually they made it known they didn't need to always hear about it. This hurt me at first because the way they went about it made me feel like I was under attack, but because I had grown as a person, I was able to try and understand that they were right in telling me how this bothered them. There are times, however, when the personal growth I have experienced so far actually makes me feel like I don't fit in with my family or other people, and I wonder if I will ever find others who, like me, are also self-actualizing. I try to remember that not everyone feels the way I do about growing as a person, and that there's still plenty of room for both personal and spiritual growth in my own life.

As a matter of fact there are still times when I do things I don't like myself for, like making crude jokes to be funny, or exhibiting some of my old sarcasm in a joking manner. And even though I love my wife and would never do anything to hurt her, I still lust occasionally. Also there are times when I get angry over little things that I feel I shouldn't, or if angry at my wife, say something I wish I hadn't. I try not to get mad at myself for these things, because I know none of it is as bad as it use to be, and because I know in my heart it's not who I am. However despite all of these things, I still try to take each day as it comes, and although I may not be happy at times on some days, I can honestly say I am happy every day of my life, because I look at the problems between me and my wife as a way to learn how to love others unconditionally and any doubts and fears I may have as opportunities to keep growing spiritually.

11

Why I Believe what I Do

I want you to understand I'm not asking you to believe what I do, just that I do and that it has made a difference in my life.

When I look back over my sobriety, if there is one thing that has led me to believe more than anything else that we can find our own answers in life and can create our own happiness, it would have to be The Twelve Steps of Alcoholics Anonymous. It was through them that I found the answers I needed to stay sober and by practicing them that I began to like myself and experience happiness like never before. However, it wasn't until after I had grown more spiritual through the practice of these steps that I was able to love myself and experience a feeling of happiness that I didn't believe possible. After doing the first nine steps as quickly as possible, I never stopped trying to practice the last three steps as best as I could. It was, in fact, those last three steps that I believe helped me the most to grow more spiritual and eventually love myself.

Here are how those last steps helped me: Step Ten. Continued to fearlessly take an inventory of myself and when wrong, admitted it right away. This step helped me to look at myself and not blame others for any of the negative emotions I still felt, and to continue to try and change the things about myself that I needed to in order to stay sober and be happy. It was also the step where I began to try and practice love, kindness, tolerance, and understanding towards others, and not be so hard on myself when I failed at it. Step Eleven. Tried with prayer and meditation to improve my conscious connection with whatever God I understood there to be, praying only to know what His will was for me and the strength to do it. This step helped me to try harder to practice love, kindness, tolerance, and understanding towards others and was where I believe I also began trying to practice these things towards myself. And although I didn't meditate through most of my sobriety, I did seek through prayer to improve my conscious contact with God, and to help me with the many fears I had throughout my sobriety. Step Twelve. Having been awakened spiritually by doing these steps, I tried to share this experience with alcoholics and to practice what I had learned in my everyday life. This step told me that although there may be a different definition of a spiritual awakening for every person who has had one, they all seem to have one thing in common—the person is now able to do, feel, and believe that which they had been unable to do before on their unaided strength and resources alone.

It was because of the Spiritual Awakening that I had that I was able to continue to stay sober, help other alcoholics, and begin feeling a love for myself and others. However, even though this spiritual awakening was also the reason I was able to get through many of the doubts and fears I had in my sobriety by relying on God to help me, it still didn't give me the complete reassurance that God really did exist.

Faith in a creator I didn't have most of my adult life. Faith in myself I never had in my teenage years. And Faith that everything was going to be all right even when it wasn't, that I so desperately needed in my childhood

Many books have been written on the subject of God, and how important it is to have faith in our lives. And quite a few have been written on how we have the ability to create our lives the way we want them to be through our thoughts and beliefs. As you know, I have read a few books that basically combined these two things, and will admit it was through them that I felt I had found the answers to some of life's most pressing questions. However, even though I felt there may be a lot of truth to what these books told me and I began relying on them along with prayer, AA meetings, and the Twelve Steps to help me feel better whenever I experienced certain fears in my life, it was what I discovered through science (the Big Bang Theory and Quantum Physics) that helped me the most with my fears by giving me the reassurance I was looking for that there had to be something that created this universe and life for a reason. The Big Bang Theory explained how the universe came into existence. And Quantum Physics, among other things, explained how all of us have the power to create our reality through our thoughts and beliefs.

This means that everything in our lives, from our health and relationships, to our emotional and spiritual well-being, and even our finances, are things we have created in our lives to be the way they are. If we need to, we can change for the better by thinking and believing we can. I must confess, though, that despite how my life has turned out today and the fact that I know I had a big part in creating it the way it is, there are still some days when I let doubts creep in that we actually do have the power to change our lives the way we want them to be, and that I really can help others. However, it's in those times that I pray for God to give me some sign that it's truly there, and ask for the guidance and reassurance I need that shows me I'm on the right track with what I have set out to do with this book. I finish by telling this God that I've found that I love it. I also remind myself once again of how much I really have played a part in becoming who I am today, and tell myself that I can help people who, like myself, have let their doubts and fears make them unhappy. People that I know would like to be happy, but never received enough guidance and reassurance in their lives to know how to be or never developed the kind of faith to believe they can be happy.

Two things I no longer believe in, as a result of my search for reassurance in some kind of creator, are the devil and hell. It just doesn't make sense to me that any kind of God would have set this world up in such a way that there has to be a constant struggle for us between good and evil, and if we don't behave exactly the way we're told to, we are going to face some kind of fiery damnation after we die. Sure, there are things that happen in this world that in no way can be called good, but to claim there is a devil at work is just something I find hard to believe. I know in my own life that I have done some things that by sheer definition could be called evil, and I wish I never would have done them, but I chose to do those things with the free will that we all seem to have here on earth, and it was almost always either my fears, insecurities, or negative emotions that were behind my decision to do something I regretted later. Of course, in my case, I was also usually drunk at the time, but I can honestly say that although I may not have been happy with who I was back then, I never thought I was an evil person.

Through The Twelve Steps of Alcoholics Anonymous, I have admitted to myself, another human being, and to God any wrongs I have committed, and have made amends to the people I have hurt. I also know I would never intentionally do something today that would hurt anyone in any way, and I hope the people I have hurt in the past have forgiven me. I believe in my heart that the God I have found has no need to forgive me because it isn't the angry, revengeful one that I have read about in the Bible. And although I still have regrets for some of my past deeds, I have truly forgiven myself.

I want to make it clear here, however, that I don't mean to mock anyone who believes differently than I do, and I want them to keep believing what they do. All I ever ask from people of different religions is to see how "belief" is the common denominator between their religions, and how it has been responsible for helping many of them be good people and do good things in their lives. Even atheists that I've met have some kind of belief; whether it is in themselves or something like the yin and yang of life. I know it has helped them be good people who do good things in their lives as well. I believe that most people can become a better person than they were before; however, I know from my own experiences that as we continue to do so, especially while faced with adversity, it helps to have some of our own beliefs.

Addiction: This can be defined as a dependence on a behavior or a substance that a person is powerless to stop. There are two different types of addictions people can have: Substance addictions, which include alcoholism, drug abuse, and smoking, and process addictions, which include things like gambling, spending, shopping, eating, and sexual activity. The key difference between the two types is that a physical addiction usually occurs with smoking, drinking, and drug use, but because there is often a psychological need with both types of addictions, I believe that any one of the process addictions can be as hard to overcome as the substance addictions. Although I'm not sure if the addiction I had that I mentioned earlier in the book where I liked trying different software security programs used to protect your computer and posting about them in a security forum would be classified as a process addiction, I can tell you it was very hard for me to finally stop doing it. Of course, there are other things that people can become addicted to like pornography, television, video games, hunting, fishing, and even their friends or spouses.

Although experts aren't certain why people become addicted to many of the things they do, some recent studies suggest a few reasons. People with process addictions will become filled with a sense of excitement before acting on their particular addiction and while participating in the addiction, a chemical change actually occurs in their brains and gives them a sense of euphoria that becomes the sole reason for wanting to do it again. I can certainly relate to this, as it was a feeling of euphoria I was looking for when I drank, and I too usually felt excited hours before I started drinking. As a matter of fact, I can remember a lot of times when just thinking about when I was going to drink again would cheer me up and actually help me to temporarily cope with any fears I had. That's why I believe that despite the fact that drug and alcohol abuse also changes a person's brain chemistry and that different types of drugs like heroin, crack cocaine, and methamphetamine can change a person's behaviors to the point that they're willing to do anything they have to in order to use these drugs, it's not always the physical addiction that drives them to drink and drug, but their fears, insecurities, and negative emotions. If not, then why do many alcoholics and drug addicts relapse after being sober for years? I feel it's because they never learned how to cope with life on life's terms, and never truly tried to change the thought processes and behaviors that contributed to their addiction in the first place.

Some people may argue this and claim that the feelings and emotions we have are hereditary and we are who we are at birth. And while I don't disagree that this can be true, I am living proof that we can change who we are and overcome our fears and insecurities even after they cause us to turn to something that becomes so addictive and destructive that it almost kills us. I will, admit though, that I was fortunate to find Alcoholics Anonymous, and if it weren't for this and the help of The Twelve Steps, I don't think I could have ever stayed sober long enough to find this out. As far as helping other people with addictions, while I certainly don't pretend to be an expert on process addictions, I know there are places that offer Twelve Step programs to help people with many of the ones I listed.

As for people with substance addictions, I will say that even if their drinking or drug use doesn't seem to be interfering with their life, they still need to ask themselves why they have to use something to help them be happy. Of course, if they're at the point where they've already asked themselves this question and have had friends and relatives tell them that they have a problem, then that person also needs to take an honest look at why they can't or won't stop. I know, however, because of my own experiences, this can be one of the hardest things to do. I was practically blind when it came to seeing how my drinking was hurting my wife and taking me away from my family, and how even after I became aware of it and knew I had a drinking problem, I still couldn't see how bad my situation really was.

Despite this, because the seed had been planted the first time around in AA, I was eventually able to make the admission I was an alcoholic and that I needed to go back to the rooms of AA for help.

I will caution, however, that for many people, it is absolutely necessary to go to a rehab so they can receive the proper care needed to break the physical addiction caused by drug and alcohol abuse, and to get the kind of emotional support they need at such an early stage of their sobriety. I have, however, talked to people who have relapsed after getting out of rehab because they didn't continue their recovery by going to AA or Narcotics Anonymous and following their respective Twelve Step programs. I know, for me, Alcoholics Anonymous was where I was able to find support from people who understood me, and along with them and The Twelve Steps, begin to believe I could stay sober and become truly happy. Which brings me to a question I ask people who want to quit using drugs and alcohol: "Are you truly happy?" I already know what the answer will be if they're totally honest with themselves. And the only things I know that can help someone overcome an addiction and become truly happy in life are to have faith that there really is something that I call God, and use the tools of prayer, people, and hope to help them. Of course, that person has to want help and it has been my experience that no matter what type of addiction someone has, if they're not truly ready to stop, they won't. Instead, they will continue down the path of unhappiness and experience the often terrible emotional pain that comes with addiction.

Alcoholism: Whether you believe it is a disease or a simple lack of control, I can tell you that I believe I am an alcoholic and I'm not ashamed to call myself one. Also, while I don't know how my life may have turned out had I not been one, I really don't care and I'm actually glad that I am an alcoholic. If not, I may never have become who I am today and most likely would have remained the frightened little boy I was inside. I also believe that it is a biological thing for some people to inherit an alcoholic gene that can be triggered in some way by the constant abuse of alcohol. I already told you how after turning eighteen I began to drink more abusively, and by the time I was twenty-two, I was in the throes of an obsessive and compulsive way of drinking that to me can only be described as alcoholism. I know there is the school of thought among some people that drinking too much is nothing more than a simple lack of control and not a disease, but I believe people who think this need to ask themselves why drinking can stick with some people and not others.

I know that there are people like me who have grown up with fears, insecurities, and negative emotions but never drink, but even if they did, they wouldn't become alcoholics. Yet there are some other people who had a fairly decent childhood, and for the most part become well-adjusted and successful adults, but yet after a few years of drinking won't stop even if they begin losing friends, family, and their happiness. Somewhere along the way, the drinking stuck because their bodies inherited an alcoholic gene from a parent, a grandparent, or a great grandparent. In my case, I don't think I ever stood a chance for drinking not sticking. Besides having all the emotions in place to like drinking once I tried it, from what my mother has told me about my grandfather, he drank every weekend and had to be led home by her older brother every time. He also could not have been very happy in life as he was sometimes verbally abusive to my grandmother, and often times physically abusive by today's standards to my two uncles, one of which, in my opinion, also drank alcoholically most of his life. My mother's dad died in his fifties from pneumonia when she was only two, and so it was actually the memories of her older sister about their father that my mom passed along to me. Nevertheless, it is enough information for me to believe that this grandfather who I never knew was what I would define as an alcoholic drinker, and proves to me, at least, that like the many other genes that science and medicine have discovered are passed along to us from generation to generation, there is also a gene that can be passed along, that at the very least, makes some of us prone to becoming alcoholics.

Obsession: The domination of one's thoughts or feelings by a persistent idea, image, desire, etc.

Compulsion: An irresistible impulse to act, regardless of the rationality of the motivation.

I feel these two words best describe why so many times in my life, even when I didn't want to drink, as soon as I started to think about how good it would feel to go out and get drunk, eventually an urge would hit me that was almost always too strong for me to overcome, and so I would go get drunk. I've told you how my fears, insecurities, and negative emotions were behind much of my drinking, but it is important for people with addictions to understand that these things are also behind the obsession we have to drink or drug. I won't argue that physical addiction is perhaps a bigger factor for the obsession that so often leads to compulsion. However, I know that whether alcoholics or addicts, we can sometimes actually find a form of comfort in just thinking about using or getting drunk, which also leads to the compulsion that hits us. Take some of the process addictions I listed, for example. While not physically addicting, the person still finds some form of comfort in thinking about their addictions, and when it becomes more constant, it leads to a compulsion for that person as well. I know that the physical addiction of drugs and alcohol can cause people to continue using them and make it even harder for them to quit. However, I truly believe that for a lot of people, their fears, insecurities, and negative emotions are what fuel the obsession that drives them to the point that they are compelled to do whatever it takes in order to run away from how they feel and escape into a world where they soon find comfort.

Fear: In the first official book published to help alcoholics stay sober, called *Alcoholics Anonymous*, it says in Step Four that alcoholics had fears because their self-reliance failed them, and even though some of them once had great self-confidence, it still didn't solve the fear problem, while in Step Four of another book published over a decade later to help higher-bottom alcoholics called *Twelve Steps and Twelve Traditions*, it states that alcoholics had unreasonable fears that their instincts for sex, material and emotional security, and a place in society wouldn't be satisfied. Although these two books seem to be in disagreement as to why alcoholics have fears in their lives, they do come into full agreement that fear was a major part of an alcoholic's life and that it has caused them much of their unhappiness. Because of my own life, I can certainly agree with what both of these books have to say about an alcoholic's fears, but I believe that everyone has fears in their lives, and that the true reason we all have them is because of doubts—doubts that everything will be all right in our lives when it's not, doubts in ourselves, and doubts that there really is a God.

Earlier, I explained how my parents fighting caused an uncertainty very early in my childhood because I never knew when a fight was going to start or how bad it would get. Although this uncertainty was the major cause of most of my fears as a child, it was the uncertainty I felt in myself as a teenager and an adult that caused most of the fears I had later on in life. I don't know how much the uncertainty I experienced in my childhood may have contributed to this self doubt, but I do know that out of any of the fears I've experienced because of it, none of them have ever compared to the fear I felt that morning I began to doubt there was a God. I already wrote how even today I can still let doubts about there being a God creep in and cause me to feel afraid, but fortunately this has been happening less and less. This is because it has never been clearer to me that something created this life and our universe for a reason, and that if it weren't for my belief in this creator, I may never have grown to believe in myself enough to write this book. All I know is that on the days when both my belief in a creator and myself are strong, I feel an inner joy that's different from any other happiness I've experienced, and any fears that crop up quickly vanish.

Insecurities: I explained how my fears and insecurities were responsible for the way I felt about myself and for most of the behaviors I exhibited throughout my life, but I want to add here that self-esteem issues played a part in this as well. Until my early twenties, I had low self-esteem. I'm not sure how evident this was when I was a child, but I know as a teenager, it was certainly obvious. I didn't have a true confidence and satisfaction in myself, and I often felt inferior to other teens. Even when I was sixteen and won the Golden Gloves, although it did give me a great deal of pride and satisfaction, it still didn't raise my confidence. Finally, at twenty four, after having been in the Army and becoming a salesman, I was able to feel a higher sense of self-esteem than before.

However, due to my insecurities, I would still feel inferior to most people. Even later in life when happy and sober, insecurities would cause me to feel inferior to some people, but fortunately, as my self-esteem grew, I would overcome most of them and eventually love myself enough to be happy with who I was. I have noticed over the past few years, however, that quite a few people, especially our teenagers who have apparent insecurities about themselves, still behave as though they have a very high sense of self-esteem. I first noticed this with some of the teenagers I worked with in the Big Brothers-like programs. I would talk to them about my experiences with insecurities and low self-esteem as a teenager and ask them if they ever felt this way. While many of them admitted to feeling insecure about themselves, only a few said they had low self-esteem. This wasn't much of a surprise to me, as some of them were reluctant to admit they had any self-esteem issues at all, but their answers to my next question did make me wonder. I would ask them if they could look in a mirror and honestly say, "I love you" to themselves. This would usually cause some of them to snicker, but more than a few would say they could. Remaining skeptical, however, I would then ask them if they were sure. Although they said yes, I wouldn't challenge them on it any further, and simply did my best to be an example of someone who had a true confidence and love for himself.

Since then, I've noticed how a lot of people with apparent insecurities still seem to have a very high sense of self-esteem, but after talking to many teenagers and adults about it, I think I've figured out why. Starting around the mid-eighties, negative and extreme changes started taking place in many of our movies, TV shows, magazines, songs, and even commercials, and as these changes kept on becoming more and more severe, over time, it ended up causing two generations of people to be filled with an egotism that belies their true insecurities. Just look how the movies and TV shows over the past twenty years or so have slowly been making things like crime, violence, loveless sex, and even drug use seem almost glamorous, and stressing that looks, money, and fame are the only things that matter in life.

Also think about how many songs that have come out since that time have steadily been glorifying sex and violence, and made the pursuit of notoriety and money seem to be the only goal one should have in life, and I'm not just talking about rap music either. Other genres like R&B and country music have songs that are filled with ego-driven lyrics that also seem to send the same message. And I don't think anyone can argue that TV commercials haven't become more extreme over the years, and studies have shown that they affect people of all ages by making them believe they don't stack up unless they use, wear, or own a certain product. Unfortunately, the negative and extreme changes don't just stop with the things I mentioned. Our video games have become increasingly more violent in nature over the years and project a sense of realism that over time can't be psychologically good for anyone who plays them. Then, of course, there's the Internet, that since the early nineties has grown and spawned things like MySpace and YouTube, that while certainly exhibiting many good things, is slowly becoming more of an outlet for individuals who need to feel like they're somebody special by showing erratic attention-seeking behaviors.

It seems that the standards for being "a better person than we were before" have been lowered today, and the standards for being someone special have been raised. Add in how the news media makes many people feel fearful through what seems at times like a bombardment of only the horrible and negative events in the world, and perhaps you can begin to understand why people act the way they do. Although I believe that everything I just mentioned can and does have an adverse affect on many of us, it affects our youth even more. Many of them have become so desensitized by all the negatives and extremes that instead of being able to feel a sense of pride in things like their academic achievements and family values, they are only able to feel proud by trying to be something they're not. I think they are being led to believe that by acting a certain way and doing certain things, they can be someone special and feel good about themselves. However, while it may seem that this helps them to love themselves and have more self-confidence, I think they end up feeling confused about who they are and feeling even more insecure. Sadly, it can even push some of them to act out at the different levels of violence we're seeing more of on the news.

Fortunately, with most teenagers this doesn't happen. But many teens, like a lot of adults today, do sometimes behave in an egotistical and offensive way to compensate for the insecurities and, in some cases, low self-esteem they feel. The rude, disrespectful, and many times hurtful behavior that they sometimes display only makes them feel worse. On the other hand, when someone tries as best as they can to be a better person than they were before, it can open up the door to the type of self-love that is needed to feel a true confidence and satisfaction in themselves.

Negative Emotions: I think everyone experiences both positive and negative emotions in their lives, and I believe that it's perfectly natural for us to do so. However, for those of us who grew up around negativity and strife, and with no guidance and reassurance in our lives, we learned to focus only on our negative emotions, and continue to do so even as adults. Our negative emotions can become so familiar to us that even when they make us feel miserable, we can actually get a warped sense of comfort from them. I remember many times in my life when I almost liked it if I was angry or sad about something and would often dwell in these emotions for hours at a time. I've learned, however, that holding on to these emotions slows down the spiritual growth I'm trying to achieve, and can even cause me to become physically ill.

Although I felt other negative emotions in my life, worry, anger, sadness, and self-pity were the ones I experienced the most, and along with resentment, were the ones that often led to me getting drunk. Fortunately, The Twelve Steps of Alcoholics Anonymous helped me to understand my negative emotions and work on handling them more maturely. The Tenth Step taught me how to practice self-restraint whenever I became angry about something, and to understand why I became mad in the first place. The Eleventh Step told me to pray and helped me to believe things would be all right whenever I was worried and sad. And the Twelfth Step showed me how helping others allowed me to get over my negative emotions more quickly. Our negative emotions affect people more than they realize. It seems many people I meet today, both young and old, despite any personal growth they may have achieved, often show signs of negative emotions and don't seem to have gratitude for anything good in their lives. I've learned how important it is to move past troubling emotions so I can feel the happiness I cherish so much today and like the many other things in my life, for that I am very grateful.

Anxiety: I don't experience much anxiety in my life anymore, but when I do, I've come to understand that it almost always stems from some old fear or emotion about some new situation. I realize, however, that for some people, it can be much more severe and they may need medication to help them with what has been termed an anxiety disorder. Although I never experienced anxiety of that degree, I can still remember how years ago after the "treadmill incident" happened, that on one particular day, I felt so worried and afraid that at one point I thought I was going to pass out. Although this feeling soon passed, I still remained anxious and afraid that day, and if I could have taken a pill to make those feelings go away, I would have. I learned later from someone in AA that what I experienced was a panic attack and, as I mentioned, I eventually went to a psychologist. Fortunately, after talking to this person, it helped me to understand that what I was feeling wasn't real and I left there with some reassurance I would be ok. I also didn't hesitate to continue praying to God to take away my fear, and going to AA meetings for help. I believe it was by doing all of this that I was eventually able to work through my anxiety and grow stronger both spiritually and as a person. Make no mistake about it; the anxiety I felt at that time in my life was so intense that at one point I actually thought I may end up going crazy.

Resentment: I can remember many times in my drinking days when I would become so resentful over something my wife said or did that I'd get an "I'll show you" attitude and get drunk at the first chance I could to punish her for what was almost always only an imagined insult. Although my intention was to hurt her, I would actually end up hurting myself by waking up the next day sick and hung over, and with regrets. Besides the resentment I felt towards her, there were times when I also felt resentful towards other people or some situation I didn't like, and sometimes I wouldn't get drunk. Instead, I would run whatever I was angry about over and over again in my head and actually fantasize how I would triumph over the person I was mad at, or change the situation to the way I would have liked it to be. Even years into my sobriety, there were times when I would still do this, but fortunately I very seldom do today. It affects my spirituality and my happiness, so I try to work through it as quickly as I can. I also know that no matter how long I've been sober, if I were ever to let any resentment I feel become too great, there's always a chance of it causing an "I'll show you" attitude that no matter how unlikely, could lead to me getting drunk and losing the sobriety I cherish today.

Ego: Throughout my drinking days, there were times when my pride and my "false sense of ego" would cause me to act out with such arrogance that it made people not want to be around me and left me with few friends. I would then let this pride and false sense of ego tell me there was nothing wrong with the way I acted and that it didn't matter what other people thought. Deep down I knew better and often felt sad and very lonely. Thankfully, I learned through The Twelve Steps of Alcoholics Anonymous that my pride and ego were responsible for a lot of my troubles, and as I kept practicing them, I was eventually able to build a truer sense of confidence in myself. However, it took working at the detention home for me to develop the kind of confidence and satisfaction I needed to start believing in myself. This hasn't come without its share of troubles though.

The brother-in-law who called me a few years ago and told me I sometimes say things that hurt people recently told me I have too much ego and even act arrogant at times. This surprised me, as I thought I was acting like I always had around him, but when he told me that some of his friends noticed it too and no longer wanted to be around me, I was even more surprised and hurt. Speechless at first, I then asked him exactly what it was that I was doing to make he and his friends feel this way. He told me that they're tired of hearing about my beliefs and views on life and I've even offended them at times. I hadn't realized that these people felt this way, but unlike the last time when he told me I was doing something wrong, I didn't start crying and agree with everything he said. He began to get angry and continued to make his point, and soon my wife and my sister-in-law started to say things to me about this too. At first I remained calm, but when all three of them kept up with what began feeling like an attack, I felt like I needed to defend myself and made some remarks about them and these friends that I wish I wouldn't have. This surely wasn't how I wanted the evening to go and I left there that night with my brother-in-law and me agreeing I just wouldn't come around anymore. That night really shook my self confidence and the next day, I needed to take an honest look at where I might be at fault and talk to a few people close to me about it, and it helped me to confirm what this was all about.

I like to compare this arrogance or, depending on who you're talking to, confidence I have, to being like a child with new toy. Because this new toy makes him happy, he keeps showing it off and seems to never grow tired with it. This child isn't trying to be malicious in any way to the other children he shows it to, but some become jealous and angry because they don't have a toy like his. On the other hand, there are some children he encounters who do have a toy like the one he has, or an even better one, and they don't see him as showing it off. They simply see him as being happy with something he takes pride in having just like they do.

I no longer feel the need to show off my new confidence, but I still sometimes do so. I know in my heart, though, that it is never my intention to hurt anyone and that there are reasons for why I can still behave this way; by expressing my beliefs and views in life it helps reinforce who I am and what I believe in, and temporarily fills the void I have of not being fulfilled in my life. It also helps me to keep believing that after this book is published, I will be able to go out and speak publicly about my beliefs and views. I'm not sure I can ever be the same person as before, but I am certain I can stop being the overconfident person that offends people and begin showing more of the love, kindness, understanding, and tolerance that also helps reinforce who I am and what I believe in.

Selfishness: If there is one thing that can go hand in hand with someone's ego, it is the selfish behaviors that can result from it. Although I don't consider myself a selfish person, at times I can be, but thankfully, because I'm aware of it, I can change this behavior. In my drinking days, I was a very selfish person and couldn't see it. Fortunately, I learned in AA that a lot of my selfish behaviors came from a self-centeredness that contributed to my drinking and that helping others was a good way for me to stop thinking only of myself. It took some time, but eventually, by helping other alcoholics, I became less selfish and self-centered, and a little happier too. Ironically, being concerned with only myself in my early sobriety allowed me to learn about all the factors that contributed to my drinking and this enabled me to help others even more. It was also this "good" selfishness that enabled me to start having more regard for myself and others, and feel a compassion and empathy for people that I never did before.

There are times, though, that I don't always do my best to show these things to others and this has been one of my biggest battles in my spiritual growth. I do, however, remember I'm not perfect and continually try harder to practice love, kindness, understanding, and tolerance. I also occasionally still attend AA meetings to help me practice these things. After all, it was there that I learned how getting out of myself and helping others enabled me to become a better person. And I know if it could do that back when I wasn't the person I am today, then it will surely help me reach a higher level of spiritual growth that my ego and my selfishness sometimes prevents me from achieving.

Insanity: I can certainly relate to the Albert Einstein definition of insanity I first heard in AA which is "Doing the same thing over and over again, and expecting different results." There were mornings after one of my nights out drinking, that no matter how much I regretted what happened, I eventually believed the next time I got drunk, it would be different. Along with this insanity, there was the suggestion in the AA literature that like many alcoholics, I was also mentally and spiritually sick, and because of the irrational behaviors I often displayed throughout my drinking days, I couldn't deny this possibility. Thankfully, in Step Two I was told that a higher power could restore me to sanity, and that if I didn't want to use God as that higher power, I could use AA instead. It was there that with the help of other alcoholics and The Twelve Steps that my sanity was restored rather quickly, but I feel it wasn't until I also began getting better emotionally that I was able to become spiritually well. I did this by doing the same things over and over again in respect to going to AA meetings and practicing the Twelve Steps, and after awhile I started getting the same results, which was happiness. Though there are still times when my ego and selfishness can hinder my spiritual growth. Because I am emotionally well today, it makes it easier for me to work through those things and not become spiritually sick like I was in my drinking days.

Hopelessness: Feelings of hopelessness come in different forms. Some people may feel it's because they're having financial problems that seem to never end, and others feel a sense of hopelessness due to emotional problems they fear they'll never overcome. Still others can feel a far worse sense of hopelessness because they're being physically or sexually abused and fear it'll never stop. As for me, I felt a sense of hopelessness through much of my drinking days, especially when after finding happiness by staying sober and being a family man for a while, I still ended up going out and drinking again. Today, the only time I feel even the slightest bit of hopelessness is when I let the media make me feel that way with all its bad news. Fortunately, this feeling is fleeting because I have learned to search for the many good things that also happen in the world. I believe if more people did this, it would give them hope that we can make our world a better place. I also believe by finding enough faith in whatever God there may be, people can find the hope they need to start believing they can overcome any unfortunate situation.

Honesty: I have to admit I wasn't always an honest person. I stole things and lied at times as a teenager and throughout my drinking days, I lied to cover up any of my self-made troubles. I lied to people about fights that never happened to make them think I was a tough guy and I even lied to myself to help make me believe I was one. I would also lie to myself that I was happy with life. Although over the last several years of my drinking I stopped getting into trouble and lying as much, I still lied to myself that I was happy. Shortly after I began going to AA, though, I learned how important it was to be honest with myself and others, and by taking a personal inventory, I learned what I needed to do in order to stay sober and lead a better life. I soon started to feel a true happiness and stopped having to lie to myself that I was happy. The "tough guy act" finally died while talking to the teenagers at the detention home the next morning after my physical altercation with one of the teens, and I don't believe this would have been possible if I hadn't learned to be honest with myself and others. I also think we can't ever find true happiness until we are honest with ourselves and tell another person about what we find in our personal inventories.

Humility: It didn't take a whole lot of humility for me to take a personal inventory and understand that I had to eliminate the worst of what AA called my character defects if I wanted to remain sober. But trust me, it did take a lot of humility and some courage to tell another person how these defects affected me and the awful things I did because of them. After I did, though, it helped take away the guilt I felt for so long and confirmed that I had indeed been honest with myself. From that point on, no matter how afraid I felt, whenever I did anything I felt I shouldn't have or was struggling with something in life, I would talk to someone in AA or share openly at a meeting about it. I have simply found that by doing so, it fills me with the humility that I need for me to continue trying be a better person than I was before and to keep growing spiritually.

Regret: It's written in the AA literature that as recovering alcoholics, we will come to a point where we no longer regret the past or wish to shut the door on it. I have obviously not shut the door on my past by writing this book. I do sometimes still feel regret about the past when it comes to my family. Although some of this comes from wishing I was a better husband, I often cry when I think about how I wasn't there for my children as much as I should have been while they were growing up. Many times I wish I could go back in time and show them more love and affection then I did, and also give them the guidance and reassurance they needed from me as a father. I realize I didn't know how to do any of that back then, and that their childhood wasn't as bad as what mine and some other children's were.

It simply makes me sad and angry, however, when I think about what they experienced as children and even as teenagers. In addition to all the arguments they heard between me and my wife, I know they felt neglected every time I broke one of the many promises I made to do something with them. Usually this was because I was hung over, but there were plenty of times when my selfishness prevented me from doing something with them as well. I would, of course, try to make myself believe I made up for it by buying them things, but inside I always felt bad. However, I refuse to dwell in the past and use the anger and sadness I feel to try and do my best to be a good father today. I also try to remember that I never asked to be an alcoholic and that I certainly never learned anything about being a good parent from my own parents. Nevertheless, it does occasionally haunt me that I wasn't a good father and never developed a strong relationship with either one of my children. I have recently reached out to them by telling them we need to spend more time together and although they both agreed to this, I know it will take time before this becomes a regular occurrence. My son still appears to have some anger about his childhood and adolescence, and despite the fact that the relationship between me and my daughter has improved since she wrote the poem for me, I feel we should be much closer than we are right now.

Fortunately, the relationship with my wife has improved and though there's still occasionally tension between us, I believe if we try to make our marriage work, it will. I also believe that my relationships with my son and my daughter will improve and eventually I will no longer cry when I think about their childhood. This is because I know I am now able to give them whatever guidance and reassurance they may need from me as a father, and that I will always try and show them the love and affection today that I still regret not showing them more of when they were growing up.

Hope: Although the basic definition for hope is to wish for something with expectation of its fulfillment, there's obviously a difference between hoping for something and believing you'll get it. When I was little, I always wished for lots of toys on Christmas and because I was spoiled, I believed I would get them. Unfortunately, being spoiled as a child and later as a teenager caused me to believe I should also have everything my way, and as I grew older, whenever things didn't go my way, I would become angry and sad about it. My negative emotions often led to my drinking but they also contributed to me not being able to ever have the kind of hope I needed to truly believe things could be all right, so I remained negative and mostly unhappy. I tried drinking to make me happy and that didn't work. Fortunately, after making the decision to go back to AA and praying to God that morning in 1996, I finally started to have hope I could stop drinking. My hopes have changed since then, and today one of my biggest hopes is that my story will help other people. If what has happened in my life since that morning is any indication of what having hope can do, then I have to believe it will.

Belief: When I look back over my sobriety, I see how the different people I met and the different events I experienced helped shape my life today. Although I think it was all meant to be, I can certainly see how I had a hand in creating my life through my thoughts and beliefs. Up until the time I was 36, my thinking was mostly dictated by my fears, insecurities, and negative emotions and it caused my life to be filled with a lot of turmoil and pain. However, as my thinking began to slowly change through the practice of The Twelve Steps, not only did my life change for the better, but so did I. Today I am beginning to believe more and more in a creator who gave us the ability to create our lives the way we want them, and even though I still wonder at times if things like fate and destiny also play a part in our lives, if there is something I have come to believe in one hundred percent, it's the need for us to have love for ourselves and others. Although I don't always like myself for some of the things I say or do, I have learned to love myself unconditionally. And although I don't always like other people for some of the things they say or do, I try to maintain some level of love for everyone, with my ultimate goal to love others unconditionally too. It goes without saying, though, that some people can be loveable, but hard to love.

Love: I know it can be hard for people to show love if they never received much of it growing up, and it can also be hard for them to accept it from others. I remember one time after telling a teenager I was working with that I loved him, he angrily asked me how I could say that when I didn't even know him. This set me back a bit, as none of the other teenagers I'd ever said it to had reacted that way, and after realizing it was actually a bit premature to be telling him this, as I had only known him for a few weeks, I wasn't sure how to respond. However, because I knew without a doubt that I did in fact love this young man like I did all of the other teenagers I ever worked with, after some thought, I began to explain to him exactly why I could say I love him.

First, I talked to him about the anger I knew he felt and told him some of the reasons for it, and then asked him if I was right. After he answered yes, I told him that my guess was that he wished he could stop feeling that way, but that he didn't know how, and asked him once again if I was right. After getting the yes I knew was coming, I told him I knew from my own experiences with anger that it sometimes makes us say and do things we later regret and it's hard to be happy when we are feeling like that. He nodded his head and after that, I told him flat out how I knew he was not happy in life because of the things he did and that I doubted he ever felt good about himself for any reason.

Then, as I saw his expression change from one of disgruntlement to one of wonderment, I asked him if he still thought I didn't know him. He immediately smiled as he realized what I had just done, and when he couldn't deny that I at least knew a part of him, I told him that's the part I can say I love. Up until this time I had never really thought about why it's so easy for me to tell troubled teenagers or other alcoholics that I love them, but after this experience I fully understood the reason for it. Because of my own life, I'm able to look past what others see as the bad parts of people and see the part of them that has felt so much inner pain and turmoil that it makes them behave the way they do. The same part I believe, if given the proper amount of love, can go a long way in helping that person learn to love themselves, and someday be able to show it and accept it from others.

Compassion: It is important to have compassion for those who are less fortunate than ourselves and to do what we can to help them. However, when it comes to helping people with addictions and emotional troubles, I have found that having compassion simply doesn't work. Some people either don't want to hear a message of hope or simply aren't ready to, and no matter how hard you try to help them, the old adage "you can only help those who want to help themselves" always holds true. If we're not careful, we can get caught up in negative emotions as a result of our inability to help this type of person and thus be prevented from helping someone who actually does want our help. Fortunately, some people out there do want help, and although it's hard not to have compassion for them, I've found that having empathy works much better.

Gratitude: This is something we all need to have if we want to maintain a higher level of happiness in our lives. I have a lot of gratitude for my sobriety, but I also try and maintain a sense of gratefulness for the simple things in my life that I sometimes take for granted, like having a roof over my head and good health. I can understand, though, how hard it would be for someone to feel grateful in their lives if they're experiencing things like financial troubles or health problems, or worse yet, if they have lost a loved one. While I certainly feel compassion for people who have troubles, my heart always goes out to those who have lost someone they cared for, especially if it was a young one. Being a parent and a grandfather, I can't imagine how someone could go through losing a child or grandchild, and it makes me cry whenever I hear of this happening. I do know people that have gone through these awful experiences, however, who over time learned to cope with these tragedies and become as well and happy as they could under the circumstances, and I've actually told these people how they inspire me to be happy and not complain about the little difficulties I face in life. I also pass their stories along to people who are going through troubling circumstances and full of doubt and fear to help them see that it's possible to make it through these difficult times.

I know even with my faith in a creator and the belief I have in myself today, I would still need help from others to get through a tragedy like I mentioned. But thankfully, I have learned from the people I know and from people in the rooms of Alcoholics Anonymous that it is possible to get through anything if you use the tools of people, prayer, and hope to help you, and for that I am definitely grateful.

Forgiveness: There are three experiences I have with forgiveness that stand out the most in my sobriety, and one of them is the most important to me today. The first one was being forgiven by the people I made amends to for any harm I had done them during my drinking days. The second one was being forgiven by my wife for all the things I had put her through in my drinking days. And the third experience, which is the one that is most important to me today, has to do with forgiving myself. Because I have forgiven myself for the things I did during my drinking days, or in the case of my wife and children the things I didn't do, I am able to forgive people who hurt me and I cannot think of anyone in my life that I have a resentment towards today.

Change: I never liked any kind of change in my life because it often made me feel fearful, especially when it put me into unfamiliar territory. The changes I went through as a person were also scary for me, but the more I changed, the less afraid I was of changes in my life. Today I've learned to accept that change is inevitable and try as best as I can to adapt, but I still don't always like it.

Growth: Due to the level of personal growth I've achieved so far in my sobriety, I very rarely display the insecure and often immature behaviors that I did in my drinking days. I can still be immature and even unspiritual at times when I decide to act like "the funny guy" but I don't worry about this affecting my spiritual growth like I used to because I know it's not who I really am. However, when I try to describe exactly what personal and spiritual growth is, it's very hard to do. Also, what one person considers to be personal or spiritual growth can be quite different from another's. For my own personal growth, the self-actualization I experienced was a result of it and helped take me to a whole other level of wanting to help others. For my spiritual growth, overcoming my fears with prayer and action took me to a whole other level of belief in a creator and myself. I also know that I still need to grow much more as a person and that I certainly have a long way to go before I'm at the level of spiritual growth that I see in some other people. But as I wrote in the beginning of this book, a part of spiritual growth is knowing you will always need to grow, and I will add that I believe a part of personal growth is realizing this even more.

Humor: Although I have made progress in not being the "funny guy" all the time, I never want to completely stop being one. It has helped me to see the humor in many circumstances that used to upset me, and I believe laughter can actually be a healing experience. Because of this, I realize today how important it is for us to be able to laugh when things go wrong, and how even more important it is for us to be able to laugh at ourselves. Being able to laugh at yourself is one of the greatest assets you can have in order to love yourself and be happy with who you are.

Happiness: I mentioned earlier how on the days when my belief in both a creator and myself are strong, I feel an inner joy that's different from any other happiness I experience, and although this is happening more and more, sometimes I do still feel sad. Usually there isn't any real basis for this sadness and I overcome it very quickly, but there are times when fears creep in as to whether or not I'm really meant to do what I want to in life, and this causes a deeper sadness that takes longer to get over. It's in those times, however, that I remind myself how all the different experiences in my life couldn't have been just mere coincidences and then ask God for the guidance and reassurance I need to believe that I am meant to help others. This usually happens through a chance meeting with someone who while sharing my experiences and beliefs with them agrees with much of what I'm saying and afterwards also agrees that our meeting wasn't just a coincidence.

Other times it happens by hearing a song that holds some personal meaning to me. And then there are those times when this guidance and reassurance comes through reading something I feel I was meant to. For example, in late 2007, while having a day where I was feeling fearful about my future and quite sad, I just happened to go to a local mall on my lunch break to look for a set of headphones for a small AM/FM Walkman radio I listened to while jogging. After finally finding a pair I liked and purchasing them, I started to feel a little hungry and on my way out of the mall, I saw a small newly opened newsstand that sold snacks, so I ventured in.

I was only about three steps inside the entrance when I happened to spot a magazine with a picture of Julia Roberts on the cover and after taking a closer look, I saw she had done an interview for it. At first I wasn't going to read it, but I thought maybe there was something in this interview that I was meant to read. It was a nice article, but nothing seemed to jump out at me until near the end when she was talking about how being a mother had brought so much happiness to her life. I liked this, as it had nothing to do with her celebrity, but it was something else she said that really grabbed my attention. She said she believed her destiny was to experience joy in her life. I stood there after reading this with tears in my eyes and although I didn't feel joy at that moment, I did start to feel happier and less fearful, and my belief that we do receive guidance and reassurance in our lives grew even stronger.

Identity: I wish more people would try to learn to love themselves and be happy with who they are. Some people may think what they do for a living defines who they are or that whatever fame, wealth, or reputation they've achieved does, while still others may think that simply being a good parent, spouse, or person defines who they are. Since my search for reassurance in some kind of God, how I define myself has changed over the years. When I think about how science has proven we are all made up of the same matter and yet not even identical twins are exactly the same, it makes me believe that although we are all different, we are also all one. I understand how we can let things define who we are and make it our identities, as I have allowed my jobs, reputation, and even my spirituality to do so in the past. However, due to the beliefs I have acquired over the last several years, it convinces me more than ever that no matter what our race, color, creed, or sexual preferences may be, we are all a part of something I call God, and this more than anything else helps define who we are.

Prayer: I have found that one very important element of prayer is to believe that our prayers will be answered, and although there have been times when it was hard for me to do so, I can't think of one time that after praying to God to help me overcome my fears that I didn't. However, there were other things I had to do as well, like asking others for help and having hope that everything would be all right. But it mostly involved trying to have as much faith as I could that there was indeed some kind of God. The definition of faith is a belief in the trustworthiness of an idea that's not been proven, and although I can't prove there is a God or that prayer truly works, because of everything that has happened in my life, I can't help but to believe in both of these things.

I know I haven't provided all the answers to life in this book because I don't have them all. I simply hope that what I've written will help people to at least be open to the idea of a creator and that perhaps the reason we're here is to grow more spiritual. I can understand why a lot of people find it hard to believe in some kind of God with all the apparent turmoil in the world today, but I know that a lot of good can also be found if we try to look for it. I also believe that something had to create life and our universe for a reason and that as long as we keep trying to grow spiritually, we will never stop believing everything is going to be all right.

Twelve Steps to help us "Believe in Ourselves"

1. Admitted that our fears, insecurities, and negative emotions made our lives miserable.

2. Came to believe that with the help of prayer, people, and hope we could overcome our fears and start to be happier in our lives.

3. Made a decision to try and believe in a creator that gave us the ability to be happy.

4. Took an honest look at our lives and what we needed to change about ourselves to be happy.

5. Talked openly and honestly with someone we trusted about things we regretted doing and the things we needed to change about ourselves.

6. Became ready to work on these changes and to start being a better person than we were before.

7. Started trying to be a better person than we were before and as a result began to like ourselves and feel happier.

8. Tried to grow spiritually to help us love ourselves.

9. Told people we have hurt that we are sorry unless it would cause more pain.

10. Continued to change what we needed to about ourselves and kept trying to grow spiritually.

11. Continued to use prayer and people to help us and give us guidance and reassurance in our lives.

12. Having grown more spiritual we began helping others and started to love ourselves enough to be happy with who we are.

12

Why I Want to Help Others

I sometimes ask myself, "Who am I to say I can help others?" At this time, I have no formal education or degree in the field of drugs and alcohol. I've only had three years experience working with troubled teenagers. And there are still moments when doubts in myself can creep in and make me feel afraid. It's at these times, however, that I remind myself how despite my lack of education, because of the life I've had and the knowledge I've obtained throughout my sobriety, I have been able to help a lot of people, and that there had to be a reason for the many changes I've gone through, especially while writing my story.

After doing this, it doesn't take long for my belief in a creator and myself to shine through, stop the doubts and fears I feel, and fill me with a sense of purpose in my life. One that I now hope is to be a voice for the thousands of people I've talked to since I began writing this book who have told me that due to all the negative and extreme changes that have taken place in our world over the years, they feel more fearful and insecure in their lives, and for the millions of other people that I know feel the same way. I have tried to believe that things aren't really as bad as our news media makes them out to be, and though I still believe this, I certainly can't deny that some things have certainly been getting worse over the years. In our country alone, statistics show that violent crime, drinking, and drug use has risen. Several different studies show that teen violence has increased, and suicides between the ages of 15 and 24 have also increased. And we're beginning to see more and more that our educational system apparently hasn't been working in a way that enables our teachers to reach out and do their best to educate all of their students. As I like to joke, Oprah

Winfrey can't carry the weight of the world on her shoulders alone, and it's going to take a lot of time and effort on the part of all of us to figure out what is needed to change things around. Although there are already people besides Oprah who have been helping others and making our world a better place, I know a lot more help is needed, and my hope is that I will be able to join them. I realize how tall an order this may seem for someone with a twelfth grade education that has only recently begun believing in himself. And I admit it scares me when I think about it actually happening. However, if I look at how my life has turned out so far and remember what I wrote over three years ago in the first chapter of this book, I believe I will be able to do it.

I have read that all of our fears are learned except for two that we're born with. The fear of falling and the fear of loud noises. Maybe the one of falling comes from not feeling secure, and the one of loud noises is just a fear of the unknown, I don't know. What I do know is that as I go through life, although I may not always feel secure, I can feel less afraid by remembering it's actually those times that make me grow stronger. And even though loud noises can still scare me, fear of the unknown is starting to scare me less. As far as any learned fears? They started in my childhood, grew into my teenage years, and stayed with me through my adult life. The only thing that I have found that helps me with my fear is faith. Faith there is something rather than nothing that created the universe and life for a reason. I call it God. And I pray to it in the shower.